Choreography and Verbatim Theatre

Jess McCormack

Choreography and Verbatim Theatre

Dancing Words

Jess McCormack
University of Bristol
Bristol, UK

ISBN 978-3-319-92018-4   ISBN 978-3-319-92019-1 (eBook)
https://doi.org/10.1007/978-3-319-92019-1

Library of Congress Control Number: 2018942009

© The Editor(s) (if applicable) and The Author(s) 2018
This work is subject to copyright. All rights are solely and exclusively licensed by the Publisher, whether the whole or part of the material is concerned, specifically the rights of translation, reprinting, reuse of illustrations, recitation, broadcasting, reproduction on microfilms or in any other physical way, and transmission or information storage and retrieval, electronic adaptation, computer software, or by similar or dissimilar methodology now known or hereafter developed.
The use of general descriptive names, registered names, trademarks, service marks, etc. in this publication does not imply, even in the absence of a specific statement, that such names are exempt from the relevant protective laws and regulations and therefore free for general use.
The publisher, the authors and the editors are safe to assume that the advice and information in this book are believed to be true and accurate at the date of publication. Neither the publisher nor the authors or the editors give a warranty, express or implied, with respect to the material contained herein or for any errors or omissions that may have been made. The publisher remains neutral with regard to jurisdictional claims in published maps and institutional affiliations.

Cover illustration: © Harvey Loake

Printed on acid-free paper

This Palgrave Pivot imprint is published by the registered company Springer International Publishing AG part of Springer Nature
The registered company address is: Gewerbestrasse 11, 6330 Cham, Switzerland

Preface

> The consequence of the single story is this: It robs people of dignity. It makes our recognition of our equal humanity difficult. It emphasizes how we are different rather than how we are similar…when we reject the single story, when we realize that there is never a single story about any place, we regain a kind of paradise. Chimamanda Ngozi Adichie (2009)

Novelist Chimamanda Ngozi Adichie warns us of the dangers of telling or consuming 'single stories', arguing that if an artist tries to tell one individual's story in one individual's voice then they risk closing off the possibility for any complex understanding. This book sets out to ask questions about how performance makers might approach this rejection of a single story through the staging of and more specifically the dancing of other people's words. How might dance and theatre come together to tell multiple stories but also in multiple ways?

What is the body's capacity to communicate? How can spoken words be translated into choreography? Physical theatre or dance-theatre practices that focus on the body and movement as a mode of communication, can provide verbatim performance makers with powerful means of disseminating information, provoking empathy and engaging an audience. For a practice that is fascinated with the translation of recorded/spoken verbal language into movement, it is notable that dance studies and performance studies researchers and choreographers working in the field of verbatim dance-theatre have had little contact with the field of translation studies. When this specific choreographic process is viewed as a translation process, from speech to body, from verbal language to corporeal text, then those concepts in translation studies which explore translation practice as a process of dialogue between translator and source text become pertinent and provide new ways to understand, articulate and participate in this choreographic practice.

This book extends personal research and professional practice in the field of verbatim dance-theatre. The upcoming chapters focus on translation as a dramaturgical device and choreographic practice and explore some of the choreographic process through which movement is created as a response to verbatim spoken language. Over the past eight years as a performer and a choreographer I have been involved in dance-theatre projects that focus on the meeting of recorded/spoken language and movement. Working as a performer for choreographer Karla Shacklock in 2008, I was introduced to the specific possibilities and difficulties of simultaneously delivering live text (taken from new writing and existing play texts), whilst performing tightly choreographed movement and counting beats, in order to maintain the verbal language and movement in a particular temporal relationship to one another and the accompanying soundtrack. I developed a distinct interest as a performer in the challenges presented through working in a way that demanded the evolution of techniques allowing an adept simultaneous performance of words and movement which, at times, consisted of significantly differing rhythms, tones and dynamics. I became fascinated with exploring the different forms of relationship can exist between spoken words and choreographed movement, and an exploration of the possibility for movement to play a number of different roles in this relationship (e.g. subversive, parodic, emotive).

Between 2009 and 2010, interested in exploring this translation process and the combination of verbal language and movement, I created *Bluebird* (McCormack, 2009), based on Vesna Maric's (2009) memoir of the same title, an account of coming to Britain as a 16-year-old refugee after fleeing the 1992 Bosnian conflict. Vesna Maric attended the initial work in progress sharing of *Bluebird* at The Cloud Dance Festival, London, and noted that it was both a strange and moving experience to see her words being danced. Maric's use of the phrase 'my words being danced' acted as a catalyst for a shift in my choreographic practice to one of exploring possible approaches to dancing other people's words.

This book deploys three modes of research concurrently: theoretical investigation, writing and analysis of choreographic practice and choreographic practice as a method of applied research. Chapters 1 and 2 employ the framework of translation studies to address the practice of staging verbatim theatre and then specifically the combination of spoken language and choreographed movement in the field of verbatim dance-theatre. Chapters 3, 4 and 5 explore some of the possible way that choreographers have and might approach the bringing together of choreographed movement and verbal language. I hope that this book will move fluidly between theory and practice. My hope is that it is clear when theory has informed practice and practice has inspired and clarified theory. This project, which intersects choreography, verbatim theatre, dance studies, translation studies, philosophy and performance studies, calls for embodied and theoretical ways of knowing to meet as collaborators.

Prominent formalist choreographer Merce Cunningham (1981) considered dance to be 'untranslatable' (in Foster 1992). As Foster (1992) explains 'for him [Cunningham], dance speaks messages in its own language that can never be repeated in another' (187). Foster suggests that scholars who wish to write about dance making and dance performance must find 'another model of dance' (ibid.), highlighting the importance of finding a model that 'permits parlance among mediums' (ibid.). The exploration of the relationship and dialogue between verbal language and movement is intrinsic to this study. Rising to Foster's challenge, 'another model of dance' is developed to demonstrate the possibility of dialogue between verbal language and choreographed movement. This model attempts to value the embodied experience of making, performing and viewing movement and the performative acts of writing about and reading about choreographed movement, and focuses on the dialogue between these different ways of understanding dance. At the centre of this book are the concepts of translation and dialogue; the translation of recorded/spoken language into movement, the dialogue between these two different modes of communication and the dialogue between source text and translator. It is important to acknowledge at this stage that movement is different from verbal language in this context. Tymoczko's definition of translation, which will be explored further in Chapters 1 and 2, as the breaking apart of something and telling it in a 'new form' (2005: 71), is useful here to emphasise the assertion that movement is a different form of language from verbal language. In fact, a central focus of this book is the consideration of the creative process in verbatim dance-theatre as a form of intermedial translation from recorded/spoken language to movement. Despite being two very different forms, dance theorist Bannerman (2014) in her article 'Is Dance a Language? Movement, Meaning and Communication' sees some value in considering similarities between written/verbal language and movement in order to understand how dance communicates meaning. She suggests that while the meanings that are communicated by language and dance are very different, the way they are structured uncovers some similarities:

> I contend that although like language dance communicates through cultural codes, it does not convey literal messages but then neither is dance dominated by a requirement for factual specificity. On the other hand, I also argue that dance is structured in a similar way to language and that categories formulated within linguistic theory are commensurate with ways in which dances are constructed. (2014: 65–66)

Bannerman highlights the concepts of vocabulary and syntax as belonging to her understanding of how both language and dance is organised:

> that *vocabulary* and *syntax* are present in dance in the way that the word vocabulary is often employed to describe the selection of specific movements, and syntax, to represent the combination or arrangement of these movements (vocabulary) into chains or phrases of dance material. (2014: 66)

This book does not include an exhaustive study of the similarities or differences between verbal language and choreographed movement, however this notion of considering how verbal language and movement are structured is drawn on in Chapters 3, 4 and 5 to explore and suggest some new choreographic practices. Some of my own choreographic exercises discussed in Chapter 4 explore how different aspects of movement (rhythm, dynamics, direction, body parts used) can respond to different aspects of spoken language (rhythm, tone, vocabulary). Verbal/written language and movement might share some small similarities, however there are many more ways in which they are different. As a choreographer I am aware that spoken language and movement communicate in very different ways and often this is why they are valuable collaborators in performance. Dance historian Laurence Loupe (2010) argues that one of the most ideas important to emerge from the development of contemporary dance was that dance is not merely a carrier of verbal language but is able to communicate in different ways. In agreement Bannerman (2014) argues that despite its difference from language, dance is meaningful, stating that, 'dance movement does not necessarily denote or refer to meaning in a literal way as do the words of a language…However dance is rich in associative meaning or semanticity' (77). Bannerman draws comparisons between dance and poetry and borrows linguist Hockett's (1977) term semanticity to explain that movement can represent something else:

> [w]hen the elements of a communicative system have associative ties with things and situations, or types of things and situations, in the environment of its users, and when the functioning of the system rests on such ties, we say that the system is *semantic* or is characterized by *semanticity*. (Hockett 1977: 141 in Bannerman 2014: 77)

An understanding of this term could help us see how movement might act as a metaphor. For example, a performer performing movement with their weight entirely on their head could possibly signify a sense of being uncomfortable or temporary or unsustainable, suggesting the phrase 'world turned upside down' or may invoke a specific childhood memory. Although I do believe that movement has the ability to explore complex character, narrative and themes, this research is not concerned with what or how movement can or cannot communicate on its own, but is focused on how verbal language and movement can become collaborators in the production of meaning. And, when brought together on stage, verbal language and movement can provide viewers an opportunity to explicitly consider their own interpretation of the performance material.

Referring to the influence of Saussure's theories and semiotics on her own understanding of how movement communicates meaning, Butterworth (2012) compares movement language to verbal/written language and suggests that while Saussure found that meaning is constructed through the creation and interpretation of signs, 'In dance, something similar applies, in that we "read" a dance by constructing meaning based on the ways in which our society has taught us to shape our actions and Perceptions' (147). Butterworth asserts that the signs created in movement are layered and made up of 'movement vocabulary, the qualities of the movement, the patterns, the context, the dancers themselves' (2012: 148). I agree that the performer's physical appearance (weight, height, ethnicity, age, costume), their facial expression, the movement they use, their posture, the use of space, floor patterns, proximity between different performers, the force through which performers move through space, the orientation/angle of the performers to each other and audience, the relationship to music, performance space and soundtrack, can all offer signs which are meaningful to an audience. But as previously acknowledged, this interpretation will be personal and culturally and context-specific. Mackrell (2004) addresses how movement is meaningful in a different way from verbal/written language by highlighting movement's ability to communicate in a sensual and visceral way:

> Movement may be more powerful and subtle than text when it comes to capturing the visceral dynamics of movement, the sensual texture of experience. But it can present only the most generalised of facts, the most obvious of symbols, the most stereotypical of narratives. (2004)

Here Mackrell suggests that movement's inability to communicate specific meaning inhibits its ability to communicate any complex narrative. In a professional choreographic context, Newson has suggested that 'words can't say everything, [neither] can movement say everything: how do you say "This is my sister" in dance?,' (Newson in Levene 2005). However, although Newson suggests that movement cannot be so specific as to communicate the precise sibling relationship of one performer to the next, as a choreographer his work has been concerned with exploring the potential for movement to explore and communicate complex narrative. When Newson began making work with DV8 Physical Theatre, he famously suggested that dance was a 'form in crisis' (in Gilbert 1999). Newson's assertion was that too many dance artists in the UK continued to focus on dance as a decorative rather than an expressive form. Newson, whose career could be described as being centred on issues of oppression, has produced work that continually fights to acknowledge that dance can be a valid way to explore complex ideas and politics. In an attempt to reject the creation of decorative choreography, Newson, who creates movement through improvisational tasks, mainly asks his performers to respond in a way that results in a movement language that might be described as a pushed body–language. Newson has explained that, tired of exploring the boundaries of physical risk in his work, the impetus for the creation process in DV8 Physical

Theatre's *Strange Fish* (1992) was to push the boundaries of what and how movement can communicate. Thus the starting point for the work was the question, 'Can dance deal with complex emotional narrative: can it be funny: can comic-tragic theatre be created through dance alone?' (Newson 1993). While I agree that movement can offer performers and viewers a unique sensual experience, I would dispute as simplistic Mackrell's (2004) assertion that movement does not have the ability to communicate complex symbols, narratives, emotions, characters and relationships. The argument that movement is unable to signify to an audience a specific intended meaning placed in the work by the choreographer does not mean that movement can only offer 'obvious symbols' and 'stereotyped narratives' (Mackrell 2004). I would argue that a visceral or sensual experience can give rise to a number of nuanced and complex meanings. My understanding of movement as a mode of communication is influenced by the work of philosopher Mark Johnston. In *The Meaning of the Body: Aesthetics of Human Understanding* (2007), he draws on the fields of phenomenology, in particular the ideas of Sheets-Johnson (1999) and cognitive neuroscience, mainly the ideas of Damasio (2003), to argue that the body and movement is central to meaning-making. Johnston offers the view that an experience and perception of bodily movement is how we as humans make sense of the world around us. He draws on theories of contemporary phenomenology to argue that as infants, before we develop verbal language, we first have to make sense of bodily movement. His theories advocate the dismissal of the division between mind and body and language and movement. He asserts that meaning which includes 'qualities, emotions, percepts, concepts, images, image schemas, metaphors, metonymies, and various other imaginative structures' (5) is not something that occurs solely in the brain as an intellectual activity, but is rooted in 'our corporeal encounter with our environment' (ibid.). Johnson's ideas assist in challenging Mackrell's position, as he suggests that an ability to understand complex narrative or nuanced symbols, even if presented through verbal/written language, is linked to our experience of bodily movement; 'meaning is shaped by the nature of our bodies, especially our sensorimotor capacities and our ability to experience feelings and emotions' (9). Therefore, if we understand that movement or embodied presence shapes meaning-making it does not make sense to suggest that movement is unable to bring about complex meaning. Yes, movement is more open and whilst I agree with Mackrell and Newson that it cannot communicate something as precise as 'this is a dancer who is the sister of this performer and was born in 1921 in Rome under an apple tree', this does not mean that it is any less able to offer its viewer nuanced and complex meanings. Are the performers in Bausch's *Kontakthof* (2010) who walk self-consciously across the stage and bare their teeth and adjust their clothes, hair and parts of their body, only portraying one-dimensional stereotyped characters? Are the numerous duets between different performers that include the moving between mechanical, tender and violent contact, offering only a stereotypical view of relationships? Whilst Mackrell might assert that it is not until later in this piece when the performers provide a collection of verbal stories of failed, passionate and unexpected love affairs that any complex narrative is offered, Johnson might argue that not only can the movement communicate complex meaning but the meaning manifested in this piece is inextricably linked to the movement performed by the performers.

Dance scholar Franko (2006) holds the position that dance performance always inhabits a cultural and political space and my own choreographic practice is rooted in a desire to explore how dance and movement can reflect and interact with the cultural, social and political contexts in which it is created. My choreographic practice is influenced by a tradition of expressionist dance-makers such as Wigman, Bausch and DV8 Physical Theatre and is located within an approach to dance that is concerned with movement's potential cultural, social and political references. My personal choreographic practice is inspired by the choreographic work of contemporary practitioners and companies who explore the relationship between spoken language and choreographed movement, such as DV8 Physical Theatre, Jasmin Vardimon, Wim Wanderkeybus, Stillhouse, Probe Dance Theatre, Stan Won't Dance, Bodies in Flight and DOT504. My choreographic practice is grounded in a belief that everybody interprets or takes meaning from the moving body. This interest in dance, not as a collection of codified movements but as a complex mode of communication, and choreographers' specific exploration of creating movement as an extension of how individuals may use their body to express themselves outside of the theatrical context, has an interesting history in the roots of German expressionist dance and the emergence of *Tanztheater*.

The influence of the work of Rudolf Von Laban (1971) which permitted the focus in dance to move away from a mere consideration of codified movement techniques to an examination of all types of movement and his interest in any body's potential to move with intention and expression, can be seen in the choreographic work of German choreographers in the late 1920s and 1930s. Laban's choreographic and theoretical body of work, focusing on the definition and separation of movement into temporal, dynamic and spatial elements, foregrounded an eruption of choreographers interested in exploring movement as a mode of expression/communication. Choreographers such as Laban and Jooss explored the potential of modern dance to play with the expression of concepts, human experience, characterisation, humour and irony. Elswit (2014) provides a powerful argument for how and why the work of these choreographers and dancers creating work under the Weimar Republic might have cultivated and enriched an understanding of movement as a mode of communication. Elswit suggests that political and social developments under the Weimar republic had a significant effect on both how an audience engaged with dance performance and on choreographic practice. She explains that during this period in Germany 'information about training and watching bodies was purchasable in affordable booklets and reiterated on the pages of popular magazines' (Elswit 2014: xiii), suggesting that this wide-spread fixation on physicality and its communication possibilities had 'trained audiences to 'read' certain meanings into physicality' (ibid.). Elswit also suggests that this changing focus on physicality informed the studio-based practice of choreographers who became fascinated with experimenting with the body's potential to explore and address social, political and moral questions and subject matter. Pina Bausch acknowledges that it was through contact with Jooss, as her teacher at the Folkwang School and later as a dancer in his company, that she came to understand that the most important question to consider was 'What have *I* got to say?' (Bausch 2007: 5). In a speech given at the Kyoto Prize award ceremony in 2007, Bausch describes her desire to further explore movement as a mode of communication that originated in her experience of working with Jooss and recalls the experience of 'crawling around on the ground' during her initial choreographic exploration in an attempt to push this investigation into new choreographic territory and to find 'why and how can I express something?' (Bausch 2007: 9). Servos (2011) identifies Bausch's move from performer into the role of choreographer for the Wuppertal Theatre as the birth of the genre of dance-theatre.

It began with controversy; in 1973 Pina Bausch was appointed director of dance for the Wuppertal theatres and the form she developed in those early years, a mixture of dance and theatre, was wholly unfamiliar. In her performances the players did not merely dance; they spoke, sang - and sometimes they cried or laughed too. But this strange new work succeeded in establishing itself. In Wuppertal the seeds were sown for a revolution which was to emancipate and redefine dance throughout the world. Dance theatre evolved into a unique genre, inspiring choreographers throughout the world and influencing theatre and classical ballet too. (Servos 2011)

This book focuses on contemporary choreographic practice situated within the field of dance-theatre, a genre that although having continued to shift and develop since 1973, still centres on an exploration of corporal expression and attempts to address Bausch's question: Why and how can choreographed movement communicate meaning? This book aims to expand this exploration to investigate the relationship between verbatim recorded/spoken language and movement and how verbatim recorded/spoken language can be placed in a meaningful double-voiced discourse with movement to highlight the polysemous and ambiguous nature of meaning.

An acknowledgment of movement's potential dialogue with its context is reflected in my choreographic practice by a desire to play with and explore how these references are made, recognising and inviting the audience to collaborate in the meaning making process. Foster's (1992) understanding of the second stage of the postmodern dance movement as the development of 'reflexive choreography' has been central to the development of my own choreographic practice. Foster (1992) uses the term 'reflexive choreography' (188) to describe a way of approaching dance which acknowledges the inevitability that movement will produce symbolic meaning or reference to other events. This study aims to place choreographic practice within Foster's definition of 'reflexive choreography'.

> Whereas objectivist dance has laid bare the conventions governing representation to allow the body to speak its own language, reflexive choreography works with these same conventions to show the body's capacity to both speak and be spoken through. (Foster 1992: 188)

Identifying 'objectivist' and 'reflexive' choreography as two separate stages of the postmodern dance movement, Foster suggests here that a focus on the medium and material of movement by objectivist choreographers such as Cunningham, raised the possibility that movement itself could be the primary subject of choreographic work in an attempt 'to allow the body to speak its own language' (ibid.). Whereas, Foster suggests that 'reflexive' choreography, with a focus on exploring how movement reflects and enters into a dialogue with the social and political contexts within which dancers and choreographers are working, is an attempt to explore 'the body's capacity to both speak and be spoken through' (ibid.). Foster draws on the examples of the Judson Church group and Grand Union to illustrate postmodern choreographic practice which is grounded in the idea that movement will always refer to other events, suggesting that this assumption resulted in 'the impulse to simultaneously represent the world in dance and to show the act of representation' (188). This understanding, that movement is a valid medium through which to explore the world around us and that choreography can focus on exploring and exposing these processes of representation, has been central to the development of this work. This book is framed by an understanding that dance does communicate and is influenced by Mackrell's (1997) assertion that you do not need any specific training to interpret dance. As a choreographer I am interested in making performance work that encourages a wide audience and is not aimed at a specific contemporary dance audience. Referring to her concern that some audiences avoid dance performance as they presume that dance contains a secret code that they have not learnt, Mackrell suggest that:

> in fact, the only basic skill that's needed for reading dance is a curiosity about the event- a willingness to let the movement play on our senses, to let its rhythms charge up our pulses and to let its pictures range around our imaginations. (1997: 1)

This book is written with an understanding that movement will produce images that will 'range around our imaginations' and is grounded in an understanding, well-articulated by philosopher Mark Johnson (2007), that 'things, qualities, events and symbols have meaning for us because of how they connect with other aspects of our actual or possible experience. Meaning is relational and instrumental' (268).

Theories and concepts developed by various translation theorists and Bakhtin are selected, explored and re-appropriated in terms of their usefulness to challenging and extending the choreographic process of creating movement as a response to recorded/spoken verbatim language.

This book draws on pertinent ideas and concepts located in translation studies and makes use of work of theorists (such as Kathryn Batchelor, Katja Krebs, Eugenia Loffredo, Manuela Perteghella, Clive Scott, Maria Tymoczko and Carol O'Sullivan) who are engaged in discourse that explores translation practice as a process of creative dialogue and 'text-making'; and that focuses on investigating the translator's creative agency. These theories are placed in dialogue with an examination of DV8 Physical Theatre's choreographic work and my own personal experimental choreographic practice in order to choreograph new ways to understand the process of creating movement as a response to verbatim recorded/spoken language. It is my hope therefore that this book offers an investigation into practical and theoretical ways of exploring the nature of meaning and ways to understand the subversive and disruptive potential of a performance text that includes the staging of verbatim recorded/spoken language and movement in a double-voiced discourse.

Throughout the book the term translation is used to refer to the process of choreographing movement as a response to verbatim recorded/spoken verbal language. This process could also be referred to as a process of adaptation, interpretation or intersemiotic transfer (Bassnett 2000; Carlson 2006; Milton 2009). However, this study chooses to use the term translation in an attempt to explore how contact with the critical perspectives, debates, pedagogies and methodologies located in the field of translation studies can challenge and enrich an understanding of a choreographic practice that engages in choreographing movement as a response to verbatim spoken/recorded language. Relevant theories and debates located in the field of translation studies are identified and explored in terms of their usefulness for extending this choreographic practice.

Bristol, UK   Jess McCormack

References

Bannerman, H. (2014). Is Dance a Language? Movement, Meaning and Communication. *Dance Research, 32*(1), 65–80.

Bassnett, S. (2000). Theatre and Opera. In P. France (Ed.), *The Oxford Guide to Literature in English Translation* (pp. 96–103). Oxford: Oxford University Press.

Bausch, P. (2007). *What Moves Me: Acceptance Speech at Kyoto Prize Award Ceremony*, Available at: http://www.inamori-f.or.jp/laureates/k23_c_pina/img/lct_e.pdf. Accessed 10 Apr 2010.

Butterworth, J. (2012). *Dance Studies: The Basics*. London: Routledge.

Carlson, M. (2006). *Speaking in Tongues: Language at Play in the Theatre*. Ann Arbor: University of Michigan Press.

Damasio, A. (2003). Feelings of Emotion and the Self. *Annals of the New York Academy of Sciences, 1001*(1), 253–261.

Elswit, K. (2014). *Watching Weimar Dance*. Oxford: Oxford University Press.

Foster, S. L. (1992). *Reading Dancing: Bodies and Subjects in Contemporary American Dance*. Berkeley: University of California Press.

Franko, M. (2006). Dance and the Political: States of Exception. *Dance Research Journal, 38*(1–2), 3–18.

Gilbert, J. (1999). The Happiest Day of My Life Review: From Eve to Deluge, via the Suburbs. *Independent on Sunday* [online]. Available at: https://www.dv8.co.uk/pages/review-independent-on-sunday-fromeve-to-deluge. Accessed 11 Dec 2017.

Johnson, M. (2007). *The Meaning of the Body: Aesthetics of Human Understanding*. Chicago, IL: University of Chicago Press.

Laban, R. (1971). *The Mastery of Movement* (3rd ed.). Boston, MA: Plays.

Levene, L. (2005). First-Person-Singular Sensation. *The Sunday Telegraph*. Available at: https://www.dv8.co.uk/pages/interview-thesunday-telegraphy-first-person. Accessed 11 Dec 2017.

Louppe, L. (2010). *Poetics of Contemporary Dance*. Translated from French by S. Gardner. Alton, UK: Dance Books.

Mackrell, J. (1997). *Reading Dance*. London: Michael Joseph.

Mackrell, J. (2004). The Power to Provoke. *The Guardian*. Available at: https://www.theguardian.com/stage/2004/jun/05/dance.music. Accessed 11 Dec 2017.

Bluebird. (Jess McCormack, 2009).

Milton, J. (2009). Between the Cat and the Devil: Adaptation Studies and Translation Studies. *Journal of Adaptation in Film and Performance, 2*(1), 47–65.

Newson, L. (1993). Lloyd Newson on Dance. *Dance Now, 2*(2), 11–13.

Ngozi Adiche, C. (2009). *Chimamanda Ngozi Adichie: The Danger of a Single Story* [Video file]. Retrieved from https://www.ted.com/talks/chimamanda_adichie_the_danger_of_a_single_story. Accessed 17 Nov 2012.

Servos, N. (2011). *TanzTheater Wuppertal*. Translated from German by Steph Morris [online]. Available at: http://www.pina-bausch.de/en/dancetheatre/. Accessed 13 Feb 2012.

Acknowledgements

Firstly, I would like to thank Dr. Katja Krebs and Professor Simon Jones for their insight, encouragement and hours of valuable discussion. I owe many thanks to my readers, Dr. Paul Clarke, Professor Jane Bacon, Dr. Catherine Hindson and Dr. Kirsty Sedgman. I would also like to acknowledge and thank some of the dancers who I worked with during the research process: Sophia Preidel, Lisa Rowley, Patrick Rowbottom, Owen Ridley-DeMonick, Tom Kindell and Tilly Webber. Thanks also to all of my inquisitive and creative students, whose questions and participation in workshops is always useful in developing my ideas.

Thank you to the wonderful women at the University of Bristol Day Nursery, who gave me the time I needed to write much of this book.

I would also like to thank Tom René and Vicky Bates at Palgrave Macmillan for their help and invitation to contribute to the Pivot Series.

I would like to extend a special thanks to Chris and Norma for reading initial drafts and for the creative conversations.

Thanks to Isaac and Maiya for arriving.

Finally, thank you to Dan — we make plans and we dance through them, shoulder to shoulder.

CONTENTS

1 Choreography as a Translation Process   1

2 Dancing Other People's Words: Verbatim Dance-Theatre   27

3 DV8 Physical Theatre's Verbatim Dance-Theatre:
  How Might Choreography Be Developed in Verbatim
  Performance?   63

4 Making Verbatim Dance-Theatre   89

5 Concluding Comments: Choreographed Dialogue   119

Index   127

List of Tables

Table 4.1	Mode	98
Table 4.2	Field, tenor, mode	99
Table 4.3	Mode in practice	101
Table 4.4	Field, tenor, mode in practice	102
Table 4.5	Bodies in dialogue	109
Table 4.6	Bidding	110

CHAPTER 1

Choreography as a Translation Process

Abstract What is the body's capacity to communicate? How can spoken words be translated into choreography? McCormack offers a summary of the relationship between translation theory and choreographic practice. Focusing on how the term translation has been used in choreographic discourse, she explores how theories located in translation studies might be borrowed and re-appropriated in order to understand the relationship between movement and source text in verbatim dance-theatre. The chapter concludes with a case study of DV8 Physical Theatre's verbatim dance-theatre performance work in order to ask if source text and choreographic translation can exist in a heteroglossic (Bakhtin 1981) relationship with each other on stage.

Keywords Choreography · Translation · Adaptation · Dance

The use of the term 'translation' has long been used by choreographers in choreographic discourse, yet little critical attention has been paid to how theories located in translation studies could be borrowed and re-appropriated in order to understand the relationship between movement and source text in contemporary dance-theatre. This chapter explores the importance of the term and concept of translation within the practice of dance-theatre and, more specifically, verbatim dance-theatre and why a distinction between the theories and concepts of adaptation and

© The Author(s) 2018
J. McCormack, *Choreography and Verbatim Theatre*,
https://doi.org/10.1007/978-3-319-92019-1_1

1

translation is neither needed nor possible within the specific field of theatre/dance-theatre. Thereafter, the chapter will then consider approaches to choreographic translation by dance-theatre practitioners (drawing on DV8 Physical Theatre as a case study), placing these alongside key concepts and debates in translation studies. Drawing parallels between the philosophical and practical issues in translation theory and choreographic practice, I will open a discussion about whether source text and choreographic translation can exist in a heteroglossic (Bakhtin 1981) relationship with each other on stage and if the device of on stage translation can offer a way to creatively perform the negotiable nature of verbatim dance-theatre.

To Translate into Dance?

If choreographing responses to verbatim recorded/spoken language can be viewed as a form of intermedial translation, from verbal spoken language to body or corporeal text, then how can this influence approaches to verbatim dance-theatre? The term and concept of translation, which has been central to the development of Western Dance-Theatre has taken on a new and more specific significance in the practice of verbatim/documentary dance. As discussed in the Introduction, the development of new and non-classical forms of dance in Europe began in the late 1920s with the emergence of *Ausdruckstanz*. Practitioners such as Mary Wigman, Kurt Jooss and Rudolph Laban all experimented with forms of expressive dance alongside the development of non-naturalistic forms of theatre, modernist art and music (Partsch-Bergsohn and Bergsohn 2003). Influenced by these earlier practitioners' rejection of the uniformity of classical movement, practitioners in 1970s Europe, such as Pina Bausch and Anne Teresa de Keersmaeker, further developed the form of dance-theatre (or *Tanztheater*) and explored the possibility of creating meaning and self-expression within dance. The *Tanztheater* movement began to break down boundaries between different art forms, with a focus on multiplicity and ambiguity, by combining and layering fragments of spoken text, movement, objects and images. This breaking down of boundaries and transition between different media introduced the concept of ideas being moved/translated from one medium to another. However, there was rarely one starting point within this work and the elements were developed organically alongside each other. For example, Bausch rarely based her work on existing text. She describes how a piece develops from her self-expression, stating that the work is 'growing within [her]' (Servos 2008: 237). In the 1980s and 1990s, companies such as DV8 Physical Theatre, Ultimavez, Volcano Theatre Company and VTOL Dance Company continued to break down the barriers between different art forms and explored the combination of language and movement in live performance. These companies began to experiment by taking source material, such as interviews (DV8 Physical Theatre, *MSM*, 1993), short stories (Ultimavez, *Mountains Made of Barking*, 1994) or Shakespeare's sonnets (Volcano Theatre Company, *L.O.V.E*, 1993), and developing choreographic processes to translate these texts into movement. These companies also became well known for confronting physicality and choreography, with a focus on taking risks (Murray and Keefe 2007). Dance-theatre and physical theatre practitioners and companies working in the UK and Europe today, including DV8 Physical Theatre, Jasmin Vardimon, Ballet C de la B, DOT 504, Fabulous Beast, Bodies in Flight, Ultimavez, Frantic Assembly and Probe, have all investigated the integration of text and choreography and have developed improvisational and devising techniques with this integration as the focus. As a result of working with, or in-between, different art forms, the term and concept of 'translation', defined as the shift between one form and another, has become central to choreographic discourse. The use of the concept 'translation' can be found in choreographers' commentary on their choreographic process. Before making a rigorous analysis of the term and concept of translation from the point of view of translation studies, I will briefly consider the term as it occurs in choreographic discourse. Commentary on the choreographic process by choreographers sees the term used to describe the choreographic process of transferring ideas/language/images into a physical language. In the examples below, dance-theatre practitioners use the term translation to describe creating choreographed movement as a response to a range of ideas, emotions, concepts, written/spoken language.

Pina Bausch, referring to how her choreographic process was enriched through making work for different cities in different countries with Tanztheater Wuppertal, including, Budapest, Palermo, Istanbul and London, uses the term 'translated' to name the process of turning this new experience into movement possibilities.

Getting to know completely foreign customs, types of music, habits has led to things that are unknown to us, but which still belong to us, all being translated into dance (Bausch 2007: 14).

Jasmin Vardimon, when interviewed about her choreography for *Lullaby* (2003), uses the term 'translated' to explain how the language and vocabulary of her subject matter, illness, was transferred to create the movement vocabulary and dynamics of the choreography.

> Your choreography is quite physical and sometimes violent, do you try to shock your audience? (ZB)
> No I just think that we are living in a quite violent world, unfortunately. I think it is a reality and I try to show that reality. The language which we use to talk about illness is a language of war, we talk about bacteria attacking our body, and the fight against it. Chemical warfare, x-rays—all the language is like warfare, so this is how I translated it to the movement, to the physicality. (Vardimon 2003, in Boden 2003)

An interview with the performers of *Justitia* (2007), published on the Jasmin Vardimon Company's website, uses the term 'translate' to ask one performer how the company found ways to use movement to communicate the emotional journey undertaken by characters in the piece. 'How do you translate these emotions into movement?' (Jasmin Vardimon Company 2007).

Promotional material for Rosie Kay's *Supernova* (2008) uses the term 'translate' to describe the move from scientific subject matter and concepts to movement and the dancers are framed as translators.

> Taking inspiration from time, space, energy and matter, Rosie Kay translates huge cosmic ideas into the physical, the personal and the emotional. Supernova is a journey of five extraordinary female dancers who translate the macro into the micro sensations inside us all. (Rosie Kay Dance Company 2011)

Promotional material for Les Ballets C de la B's *Lisi Estaras' primero* (2010) uses 'translate' to explain the transformation from an idea surrounding a psychological state of mind into movement.

> This intimate work mixes dance and text as the personal experiences of five performers are interweaved with children's stories. Intrigued by the way a child's mind can naturally jump from one thought to another, unpredictable and seemingly without logic, Estaras will attempt to translate this state into movement. (Les Ballets C de la B 2010)

The press release for *The Ballet of Sam Hogue & Augustus Benjamin* (2011) explains that the performance piece translates their source material into a physical language.

'*The Ballet of Sam Hogue & Augustus Benjamin* is an action of embodiment, in which emotions, thoughts and images are processed and translated in a perceptible, physical reality' (Maia and Steyaert 2011).

When Lloyd Newson began work with his company, DV8 Physical Theatre, on the verbatim productions *To Be Straight With You* (2007–2009) and *Can We Talk About This* (2011–2012), the concept of translation became a dominant feature of how the pieces were explained from the point of view of the artists involved. During this time, the term translation in respect of verbatim dance-theatre developed a new significance. The simultaneous staging of spoken text and choreography results in a specific focus on the concept of translation. With this shift in choreographic process, Newson makes a clear link between linguistics and movement by translating the words, rhythm and tone of the spoken interview into a combination of spoken word, gesture and choreography.

Interestingly, there are also some examples of translation theorists and writers who have drawn on the concept or image of the body or movement in their discussion of the translation process. John Berger in his article for *The Guardian* newspaper 'Writing is an off-shoot of something deeper' reflects on the practice of translation and uses the concept of the body to explain his understanding of the translation process,

> True translation demands a return to the pre-verbal…One then gathers up what one has found there and takes this quivering almost wordless "thing" and places it behind the language it needs to be translated into… A spoken language is a body, a living creature, whose physiognomy is verbal and whose visceral functions are linguistic. And this creature's home is the inarticulate as well as the articulate. (Berger 2014)

Here, Berger makes use of the concept of the body and movement to make his point that a translation is not a binary relationship between two languages, but a much more complex encounter between languages, cultures and the writer. Clive Scott (2000: xi), however, in the 'Introduction' to Mollett, Nikolaou and Watz's (eds) *Norwich Papers, Studies in Literary Translation, Translation and Creativity*, suggests that the translation process allows the translator 'to embody an experience of reading'. Here, Scott employs the concept of the body to explore and articulate his understanding of the translation process as that of a dialogue between source text and translator, in which the translator must step into and experience the work.

In order to deepen an understanding of the encounter between words and movement in the choreographic process within the context of verbatim dance-theatre, I will look to theories and debates located in translation studies and seek to place theory and practice in a reciprocal conversation.

Translation/Adaptation: Is There a Difference?

It is important at this stage to note the acknowledgement that choreography/movement vocabulary is not a recognised language and that the move between spoken text and choreography might be more commonly viewed as an intersemiotic transfer (Bassnett 2000; Carlson 2006; Milton 2009) rather than a translation. The decision to frame the re-writing of spoken language into choreographic language as a translation is in line with some performance scholars' view that 'any process of page-to-stage transition involves a certain level of translation or adaptation, even if no translation from another language is involved' (Radosavljevic 2007: 65). *Translation* is a word that is used in the field of dance-theatre to address something other than an interlingual transfer between two separate verbal sign systems. Translation theorists are working towards broadening the field of translation studies to include expanding definitions of translation. Tymoczko (2007) confronts Western modes of defining translations by looking to examples of 'cultural equivalents of translation' such as the Igbo words *tapia* and *kowa* which 'both have the sense break it up and tell it (in a)' (Tymoczko 2007: 71). She also cites examples 'in the various languages of India: anuvad (literally 'following after'), rupantar ('change in form'), and chaya ('shadow', used of very literal translations)' (Tymoczko 2007: 68–70). A brief consideration of UK dictionary definitions of translation in 2012 show that these definitions have expanded to include:

To take across; to interpret; to express in another medium; to transform; to express; to change from one form, function, or state to another, to retransmit; to convert; to express or explain in simple or less technical language; to move or carry from one place or position to another; change in form; speaking after; following; to tell a story across; turning over; somersault; flip; interpretation; exchange.

Broadening the definition of translation enables the change in form from word to movement to be viewed as a translation. Although a significant number of dance-theatre practitioners explore the change in form from words to movement, performance, adaptation or translation scholars have not, so far, engaged significantly in considering this process. Aaltonen (2000) proposes that translation studies, specifically in relation to translations in performance, widen its focus to include different forms of theatre, explaining that text-centred theatre is only one form of theatre. So, while the study of drama translation and theatre translation in particular, concentrates as a rule on the dominant logocentric tradition in the West, it would not necessarily have to do so (Aaltonen 2000: 20). It therefore seems appropriate to consider theoretical and practical approaches to investigate translation in relation to movement-based theatre.

Theories located in translation studies and cultural studies can be drawn upon and re-appropriated to inform, complicate and extend an understanding of the encounter between a source text and its translation, specifically into movement. In order to explain why theories located in translation studies and adaptation studies are drawn on without distinction throughout this project, a discussion surrounding the two terms and the impossibility of separation will be opened up. It has been widely acknowledged by adaptation and translation theorists that, in the field of theatre/dance, the terms adaptation and translation pose numerous problems of definition (Aaltonen 2000; Bassnett 2000; Berman 1996; Radosavljevic 2007; Perteghella 2008; Milton 2009). The terms and concepts are loosely defined in translation studies, and even more loosely defined within theatre/dance and translation practice.

The practice of deconstruction and semiotic discourse, with their arguments against any stable ground for meaning, have pervaded translation theory and had a profound effect to the extent that studies which focus on transferring literal/stable meaning within a source text to a target text now have little relevance. Bassnett observes that, when engaging with translation in the theatre, terms such as 'versions' or 'adaptation' are used to explain the process or product of translated texts (Bassnett 2000: 100). Aaltonen (2000: 75) asserts that the two processes are specifically linked in the theatre, illustrating that 'translations for the stage probably employ adaptation more frequently than does printed literature, and it can be used in theatre translation at times or with texts where it would not be acceptable in the literary system'. While Bassnett (2000) and Aaltonen (2000) argue that what may have typically been termed a translation in the theatre should also be viewed to include adaptation, Radosavljevic (2007) adds that what may be typically understood as an adaptation in theatre should also be termed a translation. Radosavljevic (2007) points out that any adaptation for live performance involves a change in form and therefore should be viewed as a translation.

> It is my belief that any process of page-to-stage transition involves a certain level of translation or adaptation, even if no translation from another language is involved. Theatre language should be understood to be distinct from the language of literature. (Radosavljevic 2007: 65)

Using the example of Alan Lyddiard's 2003 stage adaptation of Wim Wenders' *Wings of Desire* (1987), for which she was company and production dramaturg and in which late 1980's Berlin was transposed into early twenty-first-century Newcastle, Radosavljevic describes the adaptation process as 'as an exercise in 'translating a city'' (Radosavljevic 2007: 57). Within this adaptation she identifies more than one type of translation. In addition to 'appropriate semantic equivalents for the film's content in relation to the medium of the stage' (Radosavljevic 2007: 66), she points to 'a number of similar transpositions on the level of narrative and character' (ibid.). Radosavljevic's assertions have informed the approach this study takes to translating *Cathy Come Home* (BBC 1966), during which the process of selecting, responding to, interpreting, adding to, remembering, re-writing and choreographing are all investigated in terms of a translation process. In terms of dance-theatre, Stan Won't Dance's *Babel* (2009–2010) can be drawn on as an illustrative example of the difficulty in using either term exclusively to describe the work. Stan Won't Dance was formed with the intention of 'creating theatre pieces that fully integrate movement, design, music and text' (Stan Won't Dance 2009). Stan Won't Dance's co-choreographers, Rob Tannion and Liam Steel, took poet and writer Patrick Neate's film for Channel 4 *Babel* (2008), a mixture of poetry, music and images, as their source text and choreographed and directed an hour long piece of live dance-theatre. As well as using the 25-minutes of poetry that Neate wrote for the film, Tannion and Steele also commissioned Neate to write some more text for their production. In the live production, Neate's poetry is performed as spoken text addressing a wide range of topics, including honour killings, youth stabbings, advertising, war and shopping, while a simultaneous translation into choreography is performed. The spoken text and its simultaneous physical translation works together to provide a visual and aural attack on the appropriation of language by advertising and the wider media and the 'way that the corporations—"marketing pigs in marketing shit"—have stolen the words that once framed authentic emotions and values, and returned them to us twisted out of all recognition' (Jennings 2010). This piece contains a number of changes in form from film/written/spoken poetry to live dance-theatre performance. These few examples of scholars engaging with the terms and concepts of adaptation and translation in the field of theatre goes some way to illustrating that a distinction between the two terms will be problematic for any study in the field of theatre/dance translation.

Scholars aiming to explore and define adaptation do so mainly in relation to the process and product of translation. For example, Perteghella (2008: 52) refers to adaptation as 'a specific translational practice' and Vinay and Darbelnet (2000: 90) describe adaptation as a 'translation procedure'. Attempts to define the term and concept of adaptation as separate from that of translation have often centred on the idea of adaptation being a 'freer' form of translation (Perteghella 2008; Newmark 1998; Vinay and Darbelnet 2000; Bastin 1998). Bastin (1998: 6) attempts to define adaptation as 'a procedure which can be used whenever the context referred to in the original text does not exist in the culture of the target text, thereby necessitating some form of re-creation'. He asserts that adaptation can be understood 'as a set of translative operations which result in a text that is not accepted as a translation but is nevertheless recognized as representing a source text' (Bastin 1998: 5). Returning here to the example of Stan Won't Dance's *Babel* (2009–2010), Steel and Tannion explored a set of choreographic devising processes with their performers to find movement that represents/resonates with the spoken text. Steel explains that when the text is fully incorporated within the creation of the choreography then good dance-theatre work emerges 'where the spoken and choreographic language are completely integral to each other' (Steel 2010). Steel asserts that 'bad' dance-theatre creates movement 'that has nothing to do with the text' (Steel 2010). A detailed exploration of the relationship between source text and movement and an interrogation into what it might mean for a source text to be 'fully incorporated' into the choreographic process forms a central aspect of this study. Discussion in Chapter 3 will consider

DV8 Physical Theatre's verbatim dance-theatre work by examining the relationship between the verbatim recorded/spoken language and its movement translation. The creation of *Cathy Come Home* (2012) and reflection on this practice will attempt to further interrogate this fundamental relationship between source text and performance text. This search for a set of choreographic processes which create movement using spoken/written text could be described as 'a set of translative operations' which resulted in a performance text that enters into a dialogue with the source text.

In her article 'Adaptation: 'bastard child' or critique?', Perteghella (2008) examines the terms adaptation and translation in the context of the theatre and addresses the questions 'How much freer should a translation be before it becomes an adaptation? And can a distinction be made at all?'. Although her article reaches the conclusion that 'it might be an impossibility to define adaptation comprehensively, and its relation to translation' she nevertheless feels it important to attempt a definition and therefore a distinction. She offers a definition of adaptation as the re-contextualisation of a text which aims to place the source text 'into new aesthetic and political configurations, within localized target cultures' (Perteghella 2008: 63). Bastin's (1998) definition uses the concept of linguistic or cultural gaps and suggests that adaptation is employed when there are no lexical equivalents of the source language/culture in the target language/culture. This idea that a movement translation in theatre can be employed to fill gaps left by the verbal language is also present in the field of dance/physical-theatre. For example, artistic directors of Frantic Assembly, Graham and Hoggett, focus on an analysis of the source text and they set up methodical improvisations or devising tasks that analyse and look for the gaps left in the text. They describe setting up a physical task in which two performers read from a script and are instructed to take a step towards the other performer if they felt their words showed warmth and a step away if they thought the words were cold, suggesting that this exercise reveals the performers' interpretations of 'what the characters really mean when they say their words' (Graham and Hoggett 2009: 206), thus providing a visual and physical representation of the relationship being played out between two characters. The movement created in the task could be used as a floor pattern to inform the spatial relationship between the performers. Graham and Hoggett suggest that an exercise such as this that uses physicality to explore and analyse the source text 'opens up the text', finds 'gaps' and enables a translation that accesses the 'richness and depth beneath the text' (Graham and Hoggett 2009: 206). Perteghella's definition does not suggest that adaptation is a solution to any gaps but that it can be defined as the translator's decision to place the source text into a new context. While there is a clear difference in how Bastin and Perteghella explain adaptation in terms of necessity or decision, both definitions are concerned with how close or distanced the target text is from the source text and therefore reach the conclusion that an adaptation is a 'freer' form of translation.

In her introductory chapter 'Introduction: Collisions, Diversions and Meeting Points' to *Translation and Adaptation in Film and Performance*, Krebs provides a dynamic way of considering any translation by asserting that 'adaptation' and 'translation' are 'quintessentially the same' (2014: 3). Similarly, rather than focusing on defining the two terms and finding a distinction, Milton (2009) address the distance between adaptation studies and translation studies in his article 'Between the cat and the devil: Adaptation Studies and Translation Studies', published in the *Journal of Adaptation in Film & Performance* (Intellect). Milton asserts that translation studies have expanded to include adaptation as an area of importance. He cites Maria Tymoczko *Enlarging Translation, Empowering Translators* (2007) as important for 'plac[ing] our traditional approach to translation within an empiricist and positivist paradigm, which has been dominant since the advent of print culture' (Milton 2009: 58). Milton stresses that Tymoczko's assertions that the practice of translation has generally been approached through an understanding of the existence of a valid and single meaning can help translation scholars to challenge and extend their understanding of translation practice. Tymoczko argues that the traditional Western concept of translation has been built on an understanding of translating the word of God in the Bible. Tymoczko suggests that this restricted understanding of translation is no longer relevant and that translation studies has broadened out to include concepts of 'representation, transfer or transmission: and transculturation' (cited in Milton 2009: 58). Milton asserts that the focus of translation studies on equivalence discredited adaptation as an important area of study. He goes on to suggest that, with the broadening out of translation studies and the rejection of the narrow concept of translation as striving for equivalence, a distinction between adaptation and translation is neither needed nor possible. Translation studies and adaptation studies can draw on and share each other's work to aid a more in depth understanding of the practice of translation. Hand and Krebs (2009) suggest that performance and theatre studies specifically play an important role in closing the gap between adaptation and translation, asserting that it is impossible to divide the two modes and warning that an attempt to do so could result in 'a narrow, western-centric definition of translation' (Hand and Krebs 2009: 4). While Perteghella, looking at the theorisation of adaptation, comes to the conclusion that the widespread use of the term adaptation to denote such differing aspects of translation in theatre practice creates problems for scholars examining practices of theatre translation, Milton (2009) and Hand and Krebs (2009) propose a move away from the task of definition and division and towards a productive relationship between the two disciplines.

If the distinction between adaptation and translation relies on deciphering what a 'freer' translation is then the definition becomes even more problematic in the field of dance-theatre. The change in language from that of written or verbal language to that of a theatrical movement-based language could sit within the realm of translation and the fact that dance-theatre situates the source text within a new aesthetic and cultural context could sit within the realm of adaptation. The opening out of the definition of translation allows an adaptation to be viewed as a translation and the theories of both can be drawn upon without distinction. Hutcheon (2006) offers a clear argument for the two modes being viewed within the same critical framework, asserting that, like linguistic transcoding, adaptation is a form of intersemiotic transposition and thus a work of translation itself. Dance theorist Gardner (2014) in her article 'What is a Transmitter' explores the term transmitter as an alternative use of the word translator to explore the role of the performer in dance performance as keeper and presenter of choreographic work. Gardner (2014) notes that the relationship between performer and choreographic work is not as simple as the performer carrying the exact choreography that originated in a choreographer's body to present to an audience, thus preserving an 'original' repertoire.

Equivalence and Dance-Theatre

Dance-theatre translations, like any form of live performance or theatre translation, often aim to achieve or are expected to add new meaning rather than replicate the meaning in a source text. Discourse surrounding translation in academia, both in regards to theatre and in its broader context, is regularly framed in terms of loss: loss of complexity, loss of meaning, loss of authorial voice. Within the practice/genre of dance-theatre, there is a focus on the combination and integration of text and choreography. This focus often results in the source text and its translation being staged simultaneously, resulting in a 'double-voiced' (Bakhtin 1981) discourse. By placing the translation in a heteroglossic (Bakhtin 1981) relationship with its source text on stage, dance-theatre enables the work to present the entangled multiplicity of meaning present in both source and target text by highlighting the existence of contradictions, gaps, expansions and conflicts. Through this practice of 'double-voicing' and staging the negotiation point of meaning the possibility arises for new meanings to be presented.

According to Hutcheon (2006), any translation in the realm of theatre is 'likely to be greeted as minor and subsidiary and certainly never as good as the "original"'. Words such as, 'tampering', 'violation', 'interference', 'betrayal' and 'infidelity' have been used in academic criticisms and journalistic reviews to attack adaptations (Hutcheon 2006). Do questions surrounding equivalence need to be addressed in relation to translations in the field of verbatim dance-theatre? Can a dance-theatre translation aim for an equivalence to its source text?

Influenced by theatre director Bertolt Brecht and choreographer Pina Bausch, dance-theatre as a genre is committed to the understanding that in order to connect with or comment on 'real'-life/feeling something must be constructed, something artificial set up. Central to the practice of dance-theatre is the belief that use of choreography, text, scenography that includes constructed images, juxtaposition, collage, discontinuity and distortion creates a dialectical space which reveals something about reality. Dance-theatre as a genre challenges the concept of a stable meaning. Dance-theatre practitioners often create work where 'the images are not didactic, they don't tell us how to feel, but open up an experience into which we need to project our own meaning in order to complete' (Climenhaga 2009: 65); practitioners use layered metaphors in favour of explicit images in order to establish a multiplicity of meaning. For example, Pina Bausch has frequently refused to comment on the meaning of her work, saying that 'everybody sees a different piece' (Bausch, cited in Stendhal 2009). And so, for instance, in *Kontakthof* (2010), Bausch's image of a fragile older woman in a bright red ball dress sitting on a child's bright plastic mechanical rocking horse at the edge of a drab meeting hall, evokes a variety of meanings for the individual viewer.

For example, the contradiction inherent in an older woman sitting on a child's toy and the tension between the drab hall and her elegant costume could suggest a moment of fun and escapism, a comment on how old people are viewed and treated or a portrayal of loneliness or madness.

This understanding of the instability of meaning is in line with translation theory that has, since the late 1970s, moved away from the narrow definition of equivalence as the ideals of equivalence, faithfulness and neutrality began to be challenged. Looking at the concept of 'equivalence', Venuti (2007) highlights the impossibility of aiming for equivalence by suggesting that a translation can 'never simply communicate in whole or in part the text that it translates; it can only inscribe an interpretation that inevitably varies the form and meaning of that text' (Venuti 2007: 29). The concept of equivalence was also undermined as translation studies engaged with philosophical concepts such as the death of the author (Barthes 1977) and deconstruction (Derrida 1967) and the concept of a single meaning became fractured. The idea that readers, or an audience, could be unilaterally positioned was questioned as theorists placed an importance on the performative act of receiving a text. The practice of deconstruction and the concept that a text does not have one correct meaning and that an author's text is just one interpretation of that text pervaded translation studies and opened up an awareness that meaning is always negotiated rather than fixed and thus cannot be directly transferred (Batchelor 2008; Pym 2010; Tymoczko 2007; Wolf 2008). Katz (1978 in Pym 2010: 30) asserts that if it is possible for two translators to arrive at different translations of the same sentence, then there is no 'fact of the matter'. Tymoczko supports this point of view that challenges the concept of a stable meaning, asserting that 'a text elicits different responses depending on the individual reader's experience, situated knowledge, and affective life, and the meaning of the text is configured differently as a result' (Tymoczko 2007: 285).

Although dance-theatre translations/adaptations are not limited by concepts of equivalence, practitioners in the field have some strong views on what a translation/adaptation from words into choreography should or should not aim for, that in some cases could be viewed as a reaction against the concept of equivalence. In an interview, I conducted with choreographer and director Pete Shenton, he explained how his interpretation of what a physical translation should achieve influenced the choreographic/devising process for Probe's production of May (2011–2012), a piece of dance-theatre translation of Tim Crouch's script written about

May, a woman living on the edge, and her relationship with Douglas, a man living in his head. Shenton explains that before the choreographic/devising process started the group were clear on their expectations in terms of translation and how this affected their process.

> We were quite clear as a group from the beginning that we did not want to interpret the words or repeat anything that the words were already saying. It just seemed pointless. We completely ignored the text for the first week and made a load of dance that had nothing to do with the text in order to have some material to rub up against it in order to create other meanings. For me this was an essential part of the process to stop us from literally interpreting the words. (Shenton 2011)

Here, Shenton provides a clear view that the choreography, when engaging in the shift in form from text to movement, should avoid the trap of aiming for a 'literal' translation and instead focus on creating 'other' or new meanings.

An article published in the *Guardian* newspaper in 2011, entitled *Lost in translation: does dancing to words work?*, provides some evidence that the reception of dance-theatre translations also extends the view of dance-theatre practitioners that a choreographic translation is failing if it seeks to merely 'double' and not open out the meanings located in the source text. The article opens with the premise that,

> Some recent productions suggest that dancing to spoken word instead of music can work. But that feels, to me, like a rarity: there is a fine line between dancing a story and merely miming its action. This latter tends to use words as narration and the dancers as props, rather than storytellers. (Turney 2011)

Here, the suggestion seems to be that attempts to 'double' the meaning of a source text is undermining choreography or dancers' ability to create meaning in their own right. Turney goes on to assert that choreographic vocabulary is very different from that of spoken language and has the potential to explore different areas of meaning.

> It is easy for the choreographer to become tied to the literal meanings of the words, thus losing other emotional resonances. A vocabulary of movement, gesture and response is surely different from a literal vocabulary, so mapping one straightforwardly to the other is likely to be plodding. (Turney 2011)

If the aim of translations within dance-theatre practice is not to find a choreographic equivalence for the source text, then what frameworks can we draw on to understand the relationship between the two?

Heteroglossia and Dance-Theatre

Discussion surrounding equivalence and dance-theatre reveals that practitioners working in the field are driven by the ambition to add new meaning to any spoken/recorded language. Therefore, a detailed examination of the relationship between the spoken/recorded language and movement in the field of verbatim dance-theatre is important. The application of the understanding that the spoken text and choreographic translation can exist in a heteroglossic relationship in performance provides a framework with which to analyse how the choreography plays a part in the performing of the negotiable nature of meaning.

In his essay *Discourse in the Novel* (1981), one of the four essays that make up *The Dialogic Imagination* (1981), Russian linguist Bakhtin used the term heteroglossia to introduce the coexistence of different types of speech, voices or languages within a single piece of work. The word heteroglossia combines the Greek words *heteros*, meaning 'different/other' and *glóssa*, meaning 'tongue/language' (Oxford English Dictionary 2017). For Bakhtin (1981), heteroglossia is concerned with including different languages, dialects or characters' voices and establishing a 'double-voiced dialogue' and its ability to articulate the intention of the author and that of a character or the multiple discourses of a community.

This concept of heteroglossia is a component of Bakhtin's (1981) writings on the 'dialogic'. Holquist (2002) identifies the central theory that forms the foundations for Bakhtinian thinking as 'dialogism', which is essentially an understanding that the 'self' only has meaning in relation to the 'other' and that an understanding of meaning is located in the dialogue between the two. Holquist suggests that dialogism is an adaptation of Einstein's relativism,

> Dialogism argues that all meaning is relative in the sense that it comes about as a result of the relation between two bodies occupying simultaneous but different space, where bodies may be thought of as ranging from the immediacy of our physical bodies, to political bodies and to bodies of ideas in general (ideologies). In Bakhtin's thought experiments, as in Einstein's, the position of the observer is fundamental. If motion is to have

meaning, not only must there be two different bodies in relation to each other, but there must as well be someone to grasp the nature of such a relation. (Holquist 2002: 19)

Therefore, because all bodies exist in relation to each other, Bakhtin recognises the dialogue between these 'bodies' as the crucial area of consideration in understanding the 'necessary multiplicity in human perception' (Holquist 2002: 21). Holquist (2002: 16) proposes that this focus on the relationship and dialogue between 'bodies' must contain a 'depriviliging' of the 'self' through the meeting and confrontation of the 'other'. Heteroglossia can therefore be understood as an endeavour to find a conscious way for the 'self' to encounter the 'other' in literature. Bakhtin's writing focused on heteroglossia as a quality of language itself, which is crucially diverse, and on what happens when heteroglossia's assortment of languages are transposed into the novel.

> When heteroglossia enters the novel it becomes subject to an artistic reworking. The social and historical voices populating language, all its words and all its forms, which provide language with its particular concrete conceptualisations, are organised in the novel into a structured stylistic system that expresses the differentiated socio-ideological position of the author amid the heteroglossia of his epoch. (Bakhtin 1981: 300)

In line with Barthes' (1977: 147) understanding that to allocate a text a single author or interpretation would 'impose a limit on that text' Bakhtin, suggests here that heteroglossia as a strategy can provide multiple perspectives, confront and disable the dominant authorial voice and corrode the concept of the existence of any 'particular' or 'concrete' single perspective. The concept of heteroglossia can be understood in relationship to the term monoglossia, a term Bakhtin used to explain the development of a single-voiced discourse or a 'unified language' which he believed was often used to support cultural and political centralisation. Bakhtin (1981: 287) asserts that any writing which remains in a 'single and unity language' cannot contain any real dialogue and is often 'authoritarian, dogmatic and conservative'. By including different voices or languages the monoglossia is immediately disrupted and a 'double-voiced discourse' is allowed to develop. It is this double-voiced discourse which is the important product of heteroglossia, and while Bakhtin (1981: 325) acknowledges that a double-voiced discourse may arise in 'rhetorical genres', he argues that if this writing stays within the parameters of a single-voiced or single-language system then 'it is not fertilized...can never be a fundamental form of discourse: it is merely a game, a tempest in a teapot'.

Although Bakhtin did not develop a substantial body of work on the heteroglossic potential of the use of the body/movement, he does comment in his essay 'Discourse in the novel' (1981) on the heteroglossia of the non-verbal language used by clowns at medieval 'local fairs'. Bakhtin (1981: 271) attacks 'Aristotelian poetics, the poetics of Augustine, the poetics of the medieval church, 'the one language of truth' of the Cartesian poetics of neoclassicism, the abstract grammatical universalism of Leibniz (the idea of a 'universal grammar') [and] Humboldt's insistence of the concrete' for what he describes as the 'centralizing' and 'unifying' of language in order to set up a 'unitary language'. He uses the example of medieval stage performances at 'local fairs', 'buffoon spectacles' and the literature of fabliaux and schwänke as examples of works of 'low-genre' art that aim instead for the disunification of language. He suggests that the physical language of the clown was a way of presenting material that was 'consciously opposed to literary language', thus establishing a mode of 'ridiculing all 'languages' and dialects' (Bakhtin 1981: 273). He also noted that the medieval literature of the fabliaux and schwänke, popular 'low genre' and affordable short stories, which contained 'no language centre' but included and played with the voices of 'poets, scholars, monks, knights and others' meant that 'no language could claim to be authentic'. Bakhtin claimed that both these devices created works which were 'parodic, and aimed sharply and polemically against the official languages of its given time'. Going on to suggest that this material 'was heteroglossia that had been dialogized'. As introduced in the introduction, Bakhtin refers to undialogised language as being 'absolute' (1981: 427), whilst asserting that for something to be dialogised it must contain and acknowledge different and perhaps conflicting perspectives. Bakhtin was interested in the fact that dialogised heteroglossia had the potential to de-privilege any one perspective in a piece of work (427).

Bakhtin's use of both a physical language and the inclusion of voices from different people occupying varying positions in society as examples of 'dialogized heteroglossia' provides a rich ground in which to consider choreographic practice in the field of verbatim dance-theatre and to investigate the potential for locating ways of approaching the work that highlights and exposes the polysemous and ambiguous nature of meaning. Carlson (1992, 2006) brings the term and concept of heteroglossia into the realm of theatre and performance. He interprets Bakhtin's term as a method of challenging the 'regularizing and canonizing forces in literature and language (monologism and monoglossia) producing the expression of multiple perspectives through contrasting voices' (Carlson 1992: 314) and suggests that there are advantages of employing heteroglossia in performance. In this discussion of the advantages and reasons for employing heteroglossia in performance, he asserts that 'one of the most important results of an author relinquishing monologistic control over a text is that the text, like life itself, becomes much more clearly open-ended' (Carlson 1992: 317). This 'open-endedness' refers to all the possible meanings available within a performance text but also includes the audience's interpretation. In his publication *Speaking in Tongues: Language at Play in the Theatre* (2006: 180–213), Carlson assigns a chapter to the incorporation of 'side texts' and identifies on stage translation as an important area for focus within live performance.

When a human or mechanical 'translator' is interposed between one language and other, it produces a third speech that is a compromise between the original content and the new form. Thus, the device for negotiating heteroglossia adds another 'voice' to the mixture (Carlson 2006: 182).

Carlson is referring here and in his chapter '*The Heteroglossia of Side Texts*' (2006: 180–213), to the on stage translation produced by the use of supertitles or sign language. While Carlson extends an understanding of language to include projected supertitles and sign language, he does not include any discussion of the use of movement and choreography.

Just as Carlson took issue with Bakhtin's exclusive focus on heteroglossia within the novel, I am arguing for the importance of the inclusion of dialogism in non-text-based theatre, i.e. dance-theatre. The development of the term, heteroglossia and its application to dance-theatre has particular relevance when we focus on translation in dance-theatre, the potential for heteroglossic disruption of the staging of the recorded/spoken verbatim language and the movement translation side-by-side in a double-voiced discourse. As Perteghella (2013) points out, the role of a translator can be placed in a dialogic context if the translator 'becomes a participant, a speaker that speaks back to the source text'. There is wide scope for this movement translation to 'speak back' to the verbatim verbal language and the movement has the potential to use juxtaposition, collage, discontinuity and distortion to promote and provoke a sense of the instability and multiplicity of meaning. As Servos (2008: 12) explains, 'dance-theatre uses a multifaceted, multilayered language of metaphors in which nuances and resonances are more important than pure description and naming'. This lack of focus on a single/specific message/meaning means that dance-theatre performance is created with the belief that the production is not the carrier, or conveyer, of meaning but rather, the provocation of meaning. The ultimate production of meaning is the responsibility of the individual viewer and thus the incongruity in performance acts as a reminder that no single point of view can prevail. The heteroglossic presentation of the text and the movement, that is the 'double-voicing' of the text and the translation of the choreographer-director/performers, is expanded to include the audience as a third interpretive body. The presentation of text and movement in a double-voiced discourse is a key characteristic within dance-theatre in stimulating wider audience participation in the understanding and use of language/translation in performance.

On Stage Translation in Verbatim Dance-Theatre

DV8 Physical Theatre's *To Be Straight With You* offers an interesting example of translation. The performance piece provides a translation of recorded interviews into a piece of dance-theatre choreography. Newson and the company initially edited the interviews into a collection of monologues, after which choreography was found for each separate scene through task-based exercises and improvisation. Newson selected specific movement from these exercises and aimed to create choreography that would support, add depth and 'illuminate' the words of the recorded interview. The majority of the performance piece sees the verbatim account and movement co-exist on stage, thus presenting the audience with the verbatim speech spoken by the performer who simultaneously performs its translation.

For example, Dan Canham performs a speech edited from an interview with a Christian man that took place as he protested outside parliament, opposing *The Equality Act (Sexual Orientation)* (2007) outlawing discrimination against lesbians and gay men in the provision of goods and services. The edited speech explores his perspective on gay adoption. In performance, Dan Canham delivers this speech, learnt from listening to the recording of the speech and attempts to perform the rhythm, accent and initiation of the recorded voice, to the accompaniment of *He Is My Story* by Arizona Dranes, one of the earliest known gospel singers.

> What we effectively have is an experiment on young people which could blow up in our faces. It's like a Frankenstein monster. We are conducting an experiment now of which the fruits will not come to some generations and is a very hasty and ill-conceived experiment. These homosexuals hanging around on street corners, waiting around for their boys and girls. Homosexuals, paedophilia, depending on how you define it, hanging around to pick them up, always in parks.

Canham sits in a chair to deliver the speech and is joined by seven others who perform tight, staccato movement with upright and inflexible posture, in exact and precise unison. During the beginning of the movement phrase, the performers' hands make their way from the chair to their hips and then move to frame their groin on the words 'Frankenstein monster', where they remain with visible tension in the hands for the rest of the scene. The use of highly structured and formalised movement supports and echoes the rigid and severe words of the speech, while the stiff, held posture could communicate the character's assumed superiority. The staccato and light footwork operates in direct contrast to the severe and serious nature of the vocabulary. As Canham delivers phrases that conflate homosexuality with paedophilia and monsters, the light, intricate and energetic footwork continues, appearing to communicate something light hearted and fun. The stiff posture of the back and the tense holding of the arms and hands, contrasted with the bouncy footwork provide a strange separation between the upper and lower body. This juxtaposition between the words and the movement performed by the lower body could imply that the speaker is possibly pleased with or unaware of the violence of the words. The tense framing of the groin throughout the movement phrase acts as a constant reminder of the speaker's conflation and blurring of the definitions of homosexuality and paedophilia. The viewer is presented with a translation that is confident in its position as a creative translation and does not appear to be confined by the concepts of fidelity or equivalence and perhaps is an example of the translator entering into a dialogue with the source text. This example also contains two different forms of communication, spoken word and movement, and at least four different voices, the words of the original speaker, the voice of the performer speaking those words, the 'voice' of the translator through the movement and the voice of the singer in the soundtrack. It is important to note that each performer may be counted as another voice as each of them performs their own 'physical voice'. Thus, the viewer is able to hear one voice expressing a violent rejection of the right of gay families to adopt children, one voice that we know is reproducing and performing these words, one voice questioning and attacking this view and one voice singing about how God is 'her story' and the only important voice. I suggest that this scene provides us with an example of heteroglossic performance material where several voices have been allowed to 'flourish' (Bakhtin 1981).

There are abundant examples of choreographers, and indeed directors, whose practice centres around the coming together of verbal language and choreographed movement. The term translation is present in a number of different ways in choreographic discourse. I have begun to examine the boundaries and interactions between translation and choreography and how theories located in translation studies might be borrowed and re-appropriated in order to consider the relationship between spoken words and choreographed movement. The next chapter will consider some of the qualities of this relationship between spoken word and choreographed movement, specifically in relation to verbatim theatre.

REFERENCES

Aaltonen, S. (2000). *Time-Sharing on Stage: Drama Translation in Theatre and Society*. Clevedon: Multilingual Matters.

Babel (Patrick Neate, 2008).

Babel (Stan Won't Dance, 2009–2010).

Bakhtin, M. (1981). Discourse in the Novel (translated from Russian by M. Holquist & C. Emerson). In M. Holquist (Ed.), *The Dialogic Imagination* (pp. 259–422). Austin: University of Texas Press.

Barthes, R. (1977). The Death of the Author. In *Image/Music/Text* (pp. 142–147). Translated from French by S. Heath. New York, NY: Hill and Wang.

Bassnett, S. (2000). Theatre and Opera. In P. France (Ed.), *The Oxford Guide to Literature in English Translation* (pp. 96–103). Oxford: Oxford University Press.

Bastin, G. L. (1998). Adaptation. In M. Baker (Ed.), *Routledge Encyclopedia of Translation Studies* (pp. 5–8). London: Routledge.

Batchelor, K. (2008). Third Spaces, Mimicry and Attention to Ambivalence: Applying Bhabhian Discourse to Translation Theory. *The Translator*, 14(1), 51–70.

Bausch, P. (2007). *What Moves Me: Acceptance Speech at Kyoto Prize Award Ceremony* [online]. Available at: http://www.inamori-f.or.jp/laureates/k23_c_pina/img/lct_e.pdf. Accessed 10 Apr 2010.

Berger, J. (2014). John Berger: 'Writing Is an Off-Shoot of Something Deeper': Language Can't Be Reduced to a Stock of Words. Most Political Discourse Is Inert and Ruthlessly Complacent. *The Guardian* [online]. Available at: http://www.theguardian.com/books/2014/dec/12/john-berger-writing-is-an-off-shoot-of-something-deeper. Accessed 12 Dec 2014.

Berman, A. (1996). Foreword. In A. Brisset (Ed.), *A Sociocritique of Translation: Theatre and Alterity in Quebec, 1968–1988* (pp. i–xvi). Translated from French by R. Gill & R. Gannon. Toronto: Toronto University Press.

Boden, Z. (2003). *Article 19 Interview: Jasmin Vardimon: Thursday 8 May 2003* [online]. Available at: http://www.article19.co.uk/interview/jasmin_vardimon.php. Accessed 9 Feb 2011.

Can We Talk About This (DV8 Physical Theatre, 2011–2012).

Carlson, M. (1992). Theater and Dialogism. In J. G. Reinelt & J. R. Roach (Eds.), *Critical Theory and Performance* (pp. 313–323). Ann Arbor: University of Michigan Press.

Carlson, M. (2006). *Speaking in Tongues: Language at Play in the Theatre*. Ann Arbor: University of Michigan Press.

Cathy Come Home (BBC, 1966).

Cathy Come Home (Jess McCormack, 2012).

Climenhaga, R. (2009). *Pina Bausch*. Abingdon: Routledge.

Derrida, J. (1967). *Of Grammatology*. Translated from French by C. G. Spivak, 1997. Baltimore, MD: John Hopkins University Press.

Gardner, S. (2014). What is a Transmitter? *Choreographic Practices, 5*(2), 229–240.

Graham, S., & Hoggett, S. (2009). *The Frantic Assembly Book of Devising Theatre*. Abingdon: Routledge.

Hand, R. J., & Krebs, K. (2009). Editorial. *Journal of Adaptation in Film and Performance, 2*(1), 83–85.

Holquist, M. (2002). *Dialogism: Bakhtin and His World* (2nd ed.). London: Routledge.

Hutcheon, L. (2006). *A Theory of Adaptation*. New York, NY: Routledge.

Jasmin Vardimon Company. (2007). *Interviews* [online]. Available at: http://www.justitiatour.co.uk/interviews.html. Accessed 9 Feb 2011.

Jennings, L. (2010). Babel: Salisbury Arts Centre. *The Guardian* [online]. Available at: https://www.theguardian.com/stage/2010/feb/21/babel-stan-wont-dance-salisbury. Accessed 9 Feb 2011.

Justitia (Jasmin Vardimon Company, 2007).

Krebs, K. (Ed.). (2014). *Translation and Adaptation in Film and Performance*. Abingdon: Routledge.

Les Ballets C de la B (2010). *Lisi Estaras' primero* [online]. Available at: http://www.sadlerswells.com/show/C-de-la-B-Baylis. Accessed 31 Jan 2011.

Lisi Estaras' primero (Les Ballets C de la B, 2010).

L.O.V.E (Volcano Theatre Company, 1993).

Maia, R., & Steyaert, T. (2011). *The Ballet of Sam Hogue & Augustus Benjamin* [online]. Available at: http://www.jardindeurope.eu/index.php?id=25&detail=302. Accessed 26 Apr 2013.

May (Probe, 2011).

Milton, J. (2009). Between the Cat and the Devil: Adaptation Studies and Translation Studies. *Journal of Adaptation in Film and Performance, 2*(1), 47–65.

Mountains Made of Barking (Ultima Vez, 1994).

Murray, S., & Keefe, J. (2007). *Physical Theatres: A Critical Introduction*. London: Routledge.

MSM (DV8 Physical Theatre, 1993).

Nettheim, M. (2008). DV8 *To Be Straight With You* [image online]. Available at: https://www.dv8.co.uk/projects/archive/to-be-straight-with-you/gallery. Accessed 1 Oct 2010.

Newmark, P. (1998). *A Textbook for Translation*. London: Prentice-Hall.

Oxford English Dictionary. (2017). *Definition of Heteroglossia in English* [online]. Available at: https://en.oxforddictionaries.com/definition/heteroglossia. Accessed 11 Dec 2017.

Partsch-Bergsohn, I., & Bergsohn, H. (2003). *The Makers of Modern Dance in Germany: Rudolf Laban Mary Wigman, Kurt Jooss*. Hightstown, NJ: Princeton Book Company.

Perteghella, M. (2008). Adaptation: Bastard Child or Critique? Putting Terminology Centre-Stage. *Journal of Romance Studies, 8*(3), 51–65.

Perteghella, M. (2013). Notes on the Art of Text Making [Blog]. *The Creative Literary Studio*. Available at: https://thecreativeliterarystudio.wordpress.com/tag/manuela-perteghella/. Accessed 6 Jan 2014.

Pym, A. (2010). *Exploring Translation Theories*. Abingdon: Routledge.

Radosavljevic, D. (2007). Translating the City: A Community Theatre Version of Wim Wenders' Wings of Desire in Newcastle-upon-Tyne. *Journal of Adaptation in Film & Performance, 1*(1), 57–70.

Rosie Kay Dance Company. (2011). *Supernova* [online]. Available at: http://www.article19.co.uk/06/feature/supernova.php. Accessed 25 Feb 2011.

Scott, C. (2000). Introduction. *Norwich Papers: Studies in Literary Translation, Translation and Creativity, 8*(1), ix–xvi.

Servos, N. (2008). *Pina Bausch: Dance Theatre*. Munich: K. Kieser.

Shenton, P. (2011, June 02). *Email to Jess McCormack*.

Stan Won't Dance. (2009). *The Company* [online]. Available at: http://www.stanwontdance.com/company/company.html. Accessed 2 May 2010.

Steel, L. (2010). Foreword. In P. Neate, *Babel* (pp. 2–4). London: Oberon Books.
Stendhal, R. (2009). *Pina Bausch: A Memory* [online]. Available at: https://www.scene4.com/archivesqv6/sep-2009/0909/renatestendhal0909.html. Accessed 20 Dec 2010.
Supernova (Rosie Kay Dance Company, 2008).
The Ballet of Sam Hogue & Augustus Benjamin (R. Maia & T. Steyaert, 2011).
To Be Straight With You (DV8 Physical Theatre, 2007–2009).
Turney, R. (2011). Lost in Translation: Does Dancing to Words Work? *The Guardian* [online]. Available at: http://www.guardian.co.uk/stage/theatreblog/2011/apr/06/dance-music-spoken-word. Accessed 31 Jan 2012.
Tymoczko, M. (2007). *Enlarging Translation, Empowering Translators*. Manchester: St Jerome Publishing.
Venuti, L. (2007). Adaptation, Translation, Critique. *Journal of Visual Culture*, 6(1), 25–43.
Vinay, J. P., & Darbelnet, J. (2000). A Methodology for Translation (translated from French by J. Sager & M. J. Hamel). In L. Venuti (Ed.), *The Translation Studies Reader* (pp. 84–93). London: Routledge.
Wings of Desire (Wim Wenders, 1987).
Wolf, M. (2008). Interference from the *Third Space*? The Construction of Cultural Identity Through Translation. In M. Muñoz-Calvo, C. Buesa-Gómez, & M. A. Ruiz-Moneva (Eds.), *New Trends in Translation and Cultural Identity* (pp. 11–20). Newcastle upon Tyne: Cambridge Scholars Publishing.

CHAPTER 2

Dancing Other People's Words: Verbatim Dance-Theatre

Abstract How do verbatim theatre practitioners explore bodies of verbatim verbal language in relation to bodies in movement? McCormack offers a detailed consideration of verbatim dance-theatre's place in the wider field of verbatim theatre. As well as addressing the emergence of dance-theatre in the field of verbatim performance, McCormack also addresses verbatim theatre makers' understanding of their creative role in a field that is repeatedly framed in terms of accuracy and fidelity. This chapter concludes by asking if an application of Bakhtin's (1981) theory of heteroglossia to explore the possibility of meaningful dialogue between the source text and translation can provide an original way to probe choreographic practice in the field of verbatim dance-theatre.

Keywords Verbatim theatre · Verbatim dance-theatre · Choreographic practice · Dialogic

> The rule is you're not allowed to create any of the words, and have to be completely faithful to the thing you're representing. (Slovo 2006)

How does dance-theatre fit into the field of verbatim theatre? Can a movement translation of the verbatim material produce a double-voiced discourse that can create creative, engaging and reflexive performance material?

© The Author(s) 2018
J. McCormack, *Choreography and Verbatim Theatre*,
https://doi.org/10.1007/978-3-319-92019-1_2

Discourse surrounding verbatim performance, like translation, is repeatedly framed in terms of accuracy and fidelity, accuracy of spoken text, fidelity of performance, accuracy of meaning. But as discussed in Chapter 1, when the already-edited verbatim text is performed in a heteroglossic relationship with the choreography on stage, this allows an audience to see the result. Through the omissions and disparity, specific emphasis and dialogue between the verbatim text and movement, the editing choices or slips in the 'faithful' transmission become visible, as does the consequence, that is the entanglement and multiplicities of meaning within both the source material (the interview material) and the presentation of that material (the performance).

Discourse encompassing verbatim theatre, especially including practitioners' own reflection on their work, is too often focused on the existence of a single truth. It is important that verbatim theatre expands its boundaries in a way which ignores established 'rules' and rejects the idea that a single or empirical meaning is something that can be determined and carefully re-located from verbatim interview to performance. It is my assertion that placing and creating verbatim performance in the genre of dance-theatre, immediately challenges this focus on a 'faithful' or 'accurate' verbatim production, includes another 'language' that disrupts the monoglossia of a performance text and opens up new possibilities for creative treatment of the material, providing new ways in which to foreground the manipulation, gaps and perspectives, resulting in rich, complex and engaging performance material. Dance-theatre's focus on collage, discontinuity and distortion to promote and provoke a sense of instability and multiplicity of meaning and its rejection of the concept of a single meaning could help tackle this focus on 'truth' that has arguably been fetishised in verbatim performance practitioners' understanding of their role and encourage theatrical creativity and innovation. Bottoms (2006: 59) asserts that performances labelled as 'verbatim theatre' 'tend to fetishise the notion that we are getting things 'word for word,' straight from the mouths of those involved'. There is an obvious tension between the discourses in translation studies explored in the previous chapter which adopt Bakhtin's theory of heteroglossia and see the translator in a creative conversation with the source text and those which focus on the 'authentic' in the verbatim performance tradition.

Monoglossic Verbatim Performance?

Will it be stools or chairs? (Edgar 2008)

Discourse surrounding verbatim performance can centre around the factual content of the work rather than a reflection on the style of theatre or aesthetics chosen by individual practitioners. Of course, performance and aesthetic considerations are not overlooked by verbatim performance practitioners. Each verbatim performance director/choreographer makes a series of complex decisions relating to how they will transform the verbatim material into a piece of live performance. These choices and theatrical strategies are often not given much space for discussion. This resonates with O'Sullivan's reflection about the fact that translators and early translation pedagogy avoided considering the translator's creative role in the translation process. The assertion that 'a translator will want the closest natural equivalent' (Niba and Taber 1966: 12) or an understanding that 'the translator's ambition is not an absolutist ambition to maximise sameness, but a relativist one to minimise difference: to look not for what one is to put into the [Target Text], but for what one might save from the [Source Text]' (Hervey et al. 1995: 17) was supported by early translation studies text books (Newmark 1988; Vinay and Darbelnet 1958) and has led to '[translation] pedagogical settings that have traditionally favoured literal approaches to textual mediation' (O'Sullivan 2012: 2). Is it possible that verbatim performance practitioners believe their role is to 'minimize difference' and that there is a problematic tension between creativity and verbatim material? Are verbatim performance practitioners locked in an understanding of their role as neutral translators, transferring meaning from interview to stage? Does this focus on authenticity, fidelity, equivalence and neutrality generate inherently monoglossic performance material? Does the inclusion of a movement translation of the verbatim material offers a possible way to open up the role of the verbatim theatre practitioner?

Gillian Slovo's (2006) question, 'At what point does the aesthetic imperative intervene in the structure of the story?' highlights the concern that too much attention to the theatrical in the staging of a verbatim piece can 'intervene' with the 'truth' of the material. In an interview with Hammond and Steward, during which Robin Soans tries to describe why and how he makes verbatim performance, he suggests that as 'those in power have grown cleverer and cleverer in news manipulation' verbatim performance offers an antidote to this as 'the audience for a verbatim play will enter the theatre with an understanding that they're not going to be lied to' (Soans in Hammond and Steward 2008: 17–19). Soans develops this line of thinking by attempting to describe how the process by which he collects an interview and transfers that experience to an audience is very different to that of a journalist.

> In verbatim theatre, the audience assumes an active rather than a passive role…Suppose I went to interview Mo Mowlam. She talks to me; I write down her words, and then edit them into a speech, or in some cases into dialogue between her and her husband. We then cast June Watson in the role. She sits on a chair on stage and talks to an audience, just as the original Mo Mowlam talked to me. By this process the audience have become me. (Soans in Hammond and Steward 2008: 23)

It is interesting that Soans introduces this as an example of the audience becoming active rather than passive because what he describes relies on the fact that at no point will the audience question the layers of selection, editing, understanding and dissemination that the verbatim material has been through. This suggestion that 'the audience have become me', that is, the interviewer or playwright, reveals Soans' portrayal of the verbatim performance practitioner's role as that of a neutral translator.

David Hare maintains that verbatim theatre is scientific rather than imaginative and uses George Steiner's assertion that it is a Jewish trait to scientifically explore the world rather than using imagination to create a new one to help explain his interest in the field and the difference between conventional and verbatim playwriting, saying 'I understand and sympathise with the idea that if the world itself is so interesting, why on earth would you want to add a layer on top of it, which is, as it were, only your own interpretation?' (Hare in Hammond and Steward 2008: 51). This assumption, that a piece of verbatim performance escapes any additional layers of interpretation during the editing, creation, rehearsal or performance process, exposes Hare's belief in the verbatim practitioner's ability to accurately and carefully transfer meaning from interviews to stage.

In an attempt to illustrate the difference between extensive research for a written play and a verbatim play, Max Stafford-Clark explains that 'what a verbatim play does is flash your research nakedly. It's like cooking a meal but the meat is left raw, like a steak tartar. It's like you're flashing the research without turning it into a play' (Stafford-Clark in Hammond and Steward 2008: 51). With this analogy we are once again presented with a verbatim performance practitioner's view that the verbatim material is allowed to be left 'raw' and untouched by the practitioners. Stafford-Clark even goes so far as to claim that the material is not turned into a play, evoking the image of a verbatim writer and directors carefully transferring each word from the interview to the stage with surgically (or professional kitchen) clean hands.

Richard Norton-Taylor explains that when he works on verbatim plays he does not view himself as an artist but rather as a journalist, therefore seeing verbatim performance as an extension of or a different mode of journalism. Whereas Soans believes that the rejection of journalism and the engagement with art will offer an audience a 'faithful' depiction of a situation, Norton-Taylor asserts that it is the dismissal of art that will enable an 'accurate' portrayal. He acknowledges that he diverges from Hare's assertion that verbatim writers are just as artistic as conventional playwrights, stating that '[e]diting-as in writing verbatim drama-may seem more of a craft than an art...I do not regard myself as an artist' (Norton-Taylor in Hammond and Steward 2008: 130). Norton-Taylor's writing about his role as a verbatim performance practitioner is imbued with references to accuracy, faithfulness and neutrality. He also believes that this journalistic approach should be equally applied to the delivery of the material by the cast, explaining that the cast for *Half the Picture* at the Tricycle, 'which soon took to the collective name of The Tribunal Players, were asked to do what they had never done before, that is, not to act in the conventional sense, but to recreate as faithfully as possible the original - the body language, the inflections, the expressions of the people they were portraying on stage' (Norton-Taylor in Hammond and Steward 2008: 128). Norton-Taylor's rejection of the concept of art and his focus on an 'accurate' and 'faithful' performance suggests a desire to view the role the translator as a neutral translator between courtroom and theatre.

Nicolas Kent, who works with Norton-Taylor, also asserts that he does not consider verbatim theatre 'art' but rather a 'journalistic response to what is happening' which he believes is the path 'to get you as near to the truth as you can' (Kent in Hammond and Steward 2008: 152–153). This focus on a journalistic and 'accurate' recreation of events leads Kent to make the bold claim that 'the strength of verbatim performance is that it's absolutely truthful, it's exactly what someone said' (ibid.). Kent asserts that verbatim performance should always aim for an 'accurate' and 'faithful' representation, arguing that verbatim work that does not do these risks distorting the truth. This resolute pronouncement that verbatim performance done in the 'correct way' can present the 'faithful' depiction of a person or situation reveals a strict understanding of his role as a neutral translator, meticulously transferring meaning from courtroom to stage.

Alecky Blythe, who believes that her difference from the majority of British verbatim practitioners is rooted in her 'ignorance' of the work going on in the field, explains that 'if you haven't read the rules, it is much easier to break them' (Blythe in Hammond and Steward 2008: 79–80). Blythe appears to think beyond the concept of carefully 'carrying across' interviews and placing them on stage by acknowledging and creatively engaging with her own and others' influence, involvement and manipulation. Blythe makes it clear that she is aware of her own agency in the creation of the performance material by saying 'I am not just a voyeur, I am also a participant' (Blythe in Hammond and Steward 2008: 79–86). Blythe describes how she managed to collect weeks' worth of verbatim material for her piece *The Girlfriend Experience* which presented the audience with verbatim material collected from the communal waiting space in a brothel,

> When I'm unable to be at the parlour myself, the girls have agreed to record themselves in my absence. This is the ultimate way of creating a non-pressurised, non-interview environment. Even so, *The Girlfriend Experience* is not a documentary and does not pretend to be one. Although my plays are created from recorded life, the characters' words have been processed at so many different stages before they reach performance that by the time they are spoken in a theatre they have taken on a life of their own. (Blythe in Hammond and Steward 2008: 93–94)

Interestingly, although Blythe could be considered to follow a more 'pure' form of verbatim practice, in that she tries to collect huge amounts of material and her cast deliver their lines by listening and repeating a live feed of the original interviews, she has a clear awareness that any verbatim material she creates is a complex tangle and a negotiation between the verbatim material and her own personal response, perceptions and emotions.

This awareness appears to have empowered Blythe in her approach to verbatim performance and rather than focusing on an 'accurate' portrayal, something she maintains is both impossible and extraneous, she has experimented with a number of different theatrical devices and modes. In 2008 Blythe stated that,

> As time has passed, I have become less literal and far less purist in my approach to verbatim. I find myself moving further away from the reality of 'how things actually happened' in my quest to create a dramatic narrative…Each attempt at crafting a narrative from recorded material has led me to bolder editing and staging, and further from the 'truth' of how it actually took place. (Blythe in Hammond and Steward 2008: 97/101)

In 2011, Blythe firmly established this conviction to move away from the restraint of an 'accurate' portrayal with her performance *London Road*, which brought verbatim performance into the realm of musical theatre. This self-reflexive piece of work that explored how verbatim material could be manipulated and transformed by music, resulted in a lively, rich, ambiguous and amazingly theatrical piece of work.

Can a focus on authenticity, fidelity, equivalence and neutrality generate inherently monoglossic pieces of live performance? Whether verbatim performance practitioners' focus on authenticity, fidelity, equivalence and neutrality allows any space for theatrical creativity or stifles experimentation is an important question. This assumption that theatre practitioners need to take care that their theatrical input does not tamper with the verbatim material, has perhaps led to verbatim performance being viewed as anti-theatrical. David Edgar (2008) suggests that, rather than wondering how the material will be presented, an audience's question on entering a verbatim play will be, 'will it be stools or chairs?'. This view resonates with Alecky Blythe's (in Lane 2010: 67) comment that verbatim performance can fall into the 'talking heads syndrome'.

Soans describes his first encounter with verbatim performance as an actor in the verbatim piece of theatre *Waiting Room Germany* (1995) written by Kalus Pohl and directed by Mary Peate, as an interesting experience, but one based in dull staging. 'In *Waiting Room Germany* we spent most of the time sitting on chairs at the front of the stage talking to the audience' (Soans in Hammond and Steward 2008: 21). Soans explains that having ascertained that most verbatim productions fall into the trap of static actors delivering 'monolithic chunks of talking' he endeavoured to be creative with the structuring of the material and attempts to splice the interviews together.

> No matter how compelling the speeches are in terms of truthfulness and revelation in their own right, the verbatim play must be more than a random collection of monologues if it is to sustain interest. In my own plays I have moved from plays that comprise a succession of monologues, to something much more complex and intricately structured, weaving strand of narrative into the source material to give it shape and make it accessible and interesting. (Soans in Hammond and Steward 2008: 26)

Soans hopes to escape presenting an arid, colourless production by being creative with the structuring of the spoken material and finding/constructing a through-line of narrative. He has also tried to find ways/situations in which to collect the interviews that will provide staging possibilities alternative to sitting in an interview chair. For example, for *The Arab-Israeli Cookbook* (2005) he collected interviews with people living in Israel and the Occupied Territories while they were cooking and then transposed this activity to the performance during which the performers prepared and cooked their dishes on stage while delivering their lines. The fact that Soans discusses the need to find alternative situations in which to collect interviews so as to find new staging possibilities, reveals his resolute commitment to stage the play as he 'found them'.

Soans also communicates a belief that verbatim theatre should unceasingly move forwards and take risks.

> I see a bright and varied future for verbatim theatre. It is my intention to maintain a degree of flexibility in this work. I have to some extent been responsible for the flourishing of the form, but success brings innovation, and fresh approaches are now springing up. This is exciting: no genre should become static or formulaic. I've hinted already at a certain reluctance to conform, and I certainly don't want to find myself hamstrung by a notion of my own making. The British love rules: 'These are the rules for verbatim theatre.' I would resist any such notion wherever possible. (Soans in Hammond and Steward 2008: 43)

Soans' own reflections on his work, even when discussing innovation and his attempts to 'break the rules' consistently uses vocabulary associated with authenticity, fidelity and equivalence and centres on the idea that verbatim theatre manages to offer its audience a glimpse of the 'truth', stating that 'artificiality is a charge that cannot be raised against the verbatim playwright unless he or she is a complete charlatan'. (Soans in Hammond and Steward 2008: 24)

Hammond and Steward's (2008) interview with Stafford-Clark and Hare focuses on the content of their work, the significance and veracity of their material with little consideration of performance elements. Stafford-Clark does observe that verbatim theatre practitioners need to find a way to elevate a performance to more than the presentation of a static actor speaking to an audience, asserting that '[t]he hard thing is to turn it into dialogue, to make the transition between somebody talking to the audience and drama' (Stafford-Clark in Hammond and Steward 2008: 51). Stafford-Clark, who works closely with the playwright Hare, believes that this challenge is best tackled in the construction of the play-text. In line with Soans comments, Hare and Stafford-Clark's approach is based on an understanding that the structuring of verbatim material into a 'dramatic' play-text supported by a metaphor that runs throughout the piece will rescue the performance from being 'boring'.

> And so you have to organise the material just as you organise the material as a playwright, to lead the audience in a certain way, through the material. And you have to have a metaphor. If the documentary play doesn't have a metaphor, just as if a purely imagined play doesn't have a metaphor or doesn't have a metaphorical element, then it's incredibly boring. (Hare in Hammond and Steward 2008: 59)

It is interesting that Hare and Stafford-Clark discuss how to avoid a static 'boring' piece of theatre by addressing only the writing of the play. Later in the interview Hare goes on to reveal his belief that performers should not experiment with the written play when he disdainfully describes a situation in which the actors had been a part of the research process, giving rise to a situation in which 'everyone thought they had the right to write' and the actors 'fell upon certain texts and felt that they were meant to pull them apart like wolves' (Hare in Hammond and Steward 2008: 53). Kent and Norton-Taylor also make it clear they are aware of the potential for verbatim theatre to produce un-theatrical boring pieces of performance. Norton-Taylor admits that 'my confidence in the theatre was not there at the beginning. Watching the early rehearsals of *Half The Picture* at the Tricycle, I thought we were heading for a humiliating disaster. How "untheatrical" it all seemed' (Norton-Taylor in Hammond and Steward 2008: 128). While Kent asserts that, 'if you are going to do a public inquiry, or a trial, most of it is incredibly boring. You take out the salient points and the most dramatic points and use those. If you did an absolutely accurate view of the trial, the audience would be bored stiff' (Kent in Hammond and Steward 2008: 152–153). Again Kent and Norton-Taylor offer very little reflection on how they overcome this in performance and the only description of performance style offered is framed in a discussion of searching for an 'exact' recreation.

Again, it is Blythe who offers very different reflections on her works, demonstrating both an awareness of this 'talking head syndrome' and a commitment to finding a creative approach to overcoming it. Blythe has on many occasions become a character in her own plays in order to find a 'technique of showing the audience how the play was made' (Blythe in Hammond and Steward 2008: 79–89). Blythe describes becoming a character in her play *Come Out Eli* (2003) after listening to the interview recording and focusing both on the man she was interviewing and on herself as a woman alone in a potentially dangerous interview situation.

> When I listened to the recording I realised that I had some great material. My journey from confident, chatty woman to scared, vulnerable girl was frightening to listen to. It took me a while to summon up the courage to let anyone else hear it, as I felt so exposed by it, and I desperately wanted to edit out the most embarrassing sections, but of course these were also the most compelling. (Blythe in Hammond and Steward 2008: 92)

Blythe's practice of placing herself as a character within the performance rejects the idea that verbatim theatre is a form of objective observation and reminds an audience they are watching a constructed situation. Blythe understands that verbatim theatre, rather than attempting to efface the theatre practitioners involved in the production and their subjectivity, needs to try to find ways to recognise and reveal the theatre practitioners place, relationship and manipulation of the verbatim material.

It is this acknowledgement that the production has a 'life of its own' which means her work is not fastened to numerous attempts at 'faithful' recreations of situations. Blythe's work has moved further and further away from literal representation, of which the verbatim musical *London Road* (2011) is a clear example. Blythe explains that as her career progressed she felt more empowered to be creative in her approach to verbatim theatre, saying that 'each attempt at crafting a narrative from recorded material has led me to bolder editing and staging, and further from the 'truth' of how it actually took place' (Blythe in Hammond and Steward 2008: 101).

Soans describes being disappointed by a 'boring' interview he conducted with a young man from the Israeli Embassy for *Talking to Terrorists* that did not make it into the final piece.

> He did nothing more than trot out the official line, learned by rote from the Embassy handbook. I knew no more at the end of the interview about him or the situation than I did at the beginning...To me, what he said wasn't new; it wasn't honest, it wasn't personal, it wasn't anchored in personal experience...Some people are boring in a fascinating or amusing way, and others are just boring. And if it's boring, it renders the whole exercise futile. (Soans in Hammond and Steward 2008: 33)

Thus, asserting that it is an individual's ability to widen, sophisticate and bring new readings into a situation that makes them interesting, 'for me someone is interesting if they widen our knowledge and complexity of the human condition, and bring fresh insight into the situations we're exploring' (Soans in Hammond and Steward 2008: 34).

Borrowing from Soans' understanding of whose interviews should make up a piece of theatre, it could be suggested that a piece of verbatim theatre which attempts to be a neutral and faithful translator can result in inherently monoglossic performance and that a successful piece of verbatim theatre needs to be brave enough to include and enmesh a personal response with the verbatim material in order to open out, complicate and encourage new readings.

Soans response to the interview with the man at the Israeli Embassy resonates with Bakhtin's interpretation of literature that aims to present a single unified voice, which he associates with promoting cultural and political centralisation. Soans suggests that the official he interviewed was unwilling to accept or acknowledge that he had and could use a different voice than the embassy's 'official line', thus speaking in what Bakhtin might refer to as to as a 'unified' or 'single-voiced' language. When watching his verbatim performance material and asserting that the audience become 'him', the person who first listened to the collected interviews, Soans appears unwilling to acknowledge that he is adding his own voice when he presents the characters' words and not presenting a 'single-voiced' dialogue. If Soans and other verbatim theatre practitioners are not interested in acknowledging, reflecting on, including or playing with their own agency in their performance material then they are inhibiting one way of developing 'dialogized heteroglossia' (Bakhtin 1981) and therefore any double-voiced discourse that may be present will remain superficial and weak in this 'unfertilized' soil.

As soon as the verbatim theatre practitioner includes and acknowledges their own voice heteroglossic material is created and a double-voiced discourse is developed. Bakhtin suggests that as soon as heteroglossia enters the novel a double-voiced discourse is set up. Bakhtin (1981: 296) provides a detailed explanation of what this double-voiced discourse can achieve below.

It serves two speakers at the same time and expresses simultaneously two different intentions: the direct intention of the character who is speaking and the refracted intention of the author. In such discourse there are two voices, two meanings and two expressions. And all the while these two voices are dialogically interrelated, they—as it were—know about each other and are structured in this mutual knowledge of each other; it is as if they actually hold a conversation with each other.

A consideration of this explanation reveals that Bakhtin believed it was important for the different voices to be aware of each other in order to hold a conversation with each other. Just as Bakhtin suggests this double-voiced discourse is 'fertilized' and given depth through the inclusion of different language, it can be seen, through the inclusion of movement or music as a different mode of communication, that the idea of a single understanding and interpretation of the verbatim material is interrupted and destabilised, creating the potential to present ambiguous, complex and rich performance material.

Can the inclusion of a movement translation of the verbatim material offer possible ways to open up the role of the verbatim theatre practitioner? With *To Be Straight With You* and *Can We Talk About This?* And *JOHN*, DV8 have demanded that this growing body of work, presented on the main stages of the UK and calling itself 'Verbatim Theatre', must include work in the field of dance-theatre. By producing verbatim work in the field of dance-theatre, DV8 have started to develop a method of presentation that immediately moves away from the accusation of 'stools or chairs' and the 'talking head syndrome' and offers a pioneering way to tackle verbatim material. I would suggest that making verbatim theatre within the field of dance-theatre offers a way to open up our understanding of the role of verbatim theatre practitioner. And as Bakhtin (1981: 273) found through his observation of clowning, the inclusion of a physical mode of communication already attacks the concept of a single and authoritative voice, by undermining the status of spoken language and presenting two modes of communication as equally important. By engaging with the process of transforming verbatim material into movement and dance, practitioners can re-focus from an accurate, faithful or neutral portrayal, to the creative treatment of the verbatim material. It is impossible for a cast of verbatim dance-theatre performers to deliver Norton-Taylor and Kent's demand for a physical recreation of the characters. Therefore, instead of asking how we can accurately portray these interviews, choreographers can ask how movement should add to/illuminate/interrogate/emote this verbatim material.

However, an examination of Lloyd Newson's reflection on his work in the field of verbatim dance-theatre reveals a practitioner also locked in a discourse about concepts of fidelity, equivalence and neutrality. Despite the fact that DV8 have been resolute in their inclusion of dance-theatre in the field of verbatim theatre, suggesting a commitment to creative treatment of verbatim material, published material by the company and interviews with Lloyd Newson reveal an ongoing concern with the abovementioned concepts. There is little room given to consideration of how the choreographic process is developed and used within this specific context, or how the choreography shifts the relationship of an audience to the verbatim material.

A letter from Newson in response to a review by Kenan Malik of *Can We Talk About This?* offers a rare and interesting insight into how Newson approached the work and how he views and articulates his role as director of a piece of verbatim dance-theatre. Newson, famous for claiming he does not read any reviews of his work, explains in this letter that he felt obliged to respond as Malik took the time to be interviewed for the production of *Can We Talk About This?*

Newson's letter to Malik includes discussion surrounding authenticity and truth and only a small section focuses on the choreographic process and the creative treatment of the collected interview material. He is responding to three areas of criticism from Malik about *Can We Talk About This?* Firstly, Malik questions the combination of movement and text, suggesting that Newson fails to find a physical equivalence to the interviews; secondly, he focuses on the fidelity of the work and its inaccurate portrayal of political figures depicted in the piece; and thirdly, he questions and criticises the subjective or unbalanced viewpoint from which he feels the piece is presented.

Malik judges the success of the translation of the verbatim material by whether the movement 'matches' the spoken word. He suggests that without finding a physical equivalence to the words a gap is opened up that prevents the audience understanding the work. Newson strongly attacks this assertion, claiming that Malik is underestimating the ability of the audience to read more than one layer of the performance and explains that his aim with this work is to demonstrate that movement can add another layer and possibly a critique of the spoken word. The quotations below illustrate this difference of opinion.

> The choreography is sublime, the movement spellbinding. Dancers contort themselves and crawl and slide and slither in a mesmerising metaphor for liberal agonies. Yet while the interaction of the dancers with each other, and with the physical space, is exhilarating, the interplay of movement and word is less so. There are times when the two fuse seamlessly. The scene in which two women, including Javinder Sanghera of the Asian women's centre Karma Nirvana, explain 'honour' violence while fluidly making and remaking themselves is quite stunning. In other scenes, however, too great a gap opens up between what is being said and what is being done. There was quite a bit of tittering during the show, because many in the audience seemed to read the dancing more as a reworking of John Cleese's Ministry of Silly Walks than as an accompaniment to a political polemic. (Malik 2012a)
>
> I have explored the relationship between text and movement for over 25 years, and firmly believe in the combined power of both to comment on and illuminate complex issues such as those explored in *Can We Talk About This?* Those in the audience who found humour ('tittering') in some of the movement are not reading the work in the wrong way, nor is it the case that humour and political polemic are mutually exclusive. A very small section of the production, in particular a scene concerning Bradford headmaster Ray Honeyford and a monologue from comedian Pat Condell, deliberately references Pythonesque movement, because at times I felt that some of the debates and hysteria around multiculturalism and Islamophobia had reached levels of absurdity. Kenan might argue that the 'tittering' of the audience implies they are not engaging with the text, but I think he underestimates those people when he assumes they can only read one element of the production at a time. (Newson in Malik 2012b)

Here, Newson demonstrates that, like Blythe, he feels empowered as a verbatim practitioner to experiment with theatrical form, play with and challenge the verbatim material in order to open-out new meanings. Newson affirms that he is not locked in an understanding of his role as a director/choreographer to find a single, fixed choreographic equivalence to the verbatim material.

Whereas, in response to the critique of the combination of movement and spoken word, Newson is forceful in his belief that verbatim material can be dealt with creatively, with regard to the criticism of his portrayal of certain political figures, Newson's response seems trapped in the vocabulary of accuracy and neutrality.

> If we were trying, as Kenan implies, to portray Honeyford as a genial, blameless hero-figure, we would not have listed some of the objectionable claims Honeyford made in his Salisbury Review article. By including strong criticism of Honeyford and considering all of the factors above, I believe we presented the situation fairly and accurately. It is important at this juncture to note that *Can We Talk About This?* is a verbatim work; all the words spoken on stage are taken from interviews and original source material. Of course there is editorial control involved in everything, but much effort has gone into cross-checking all final edits to ensure that they remain true to what was said in each interview. It is wrong and dangerous to conflate the opinions of the characters with those of DV8 or myself without recognising that throughout the work the characters are continually expressing opinions diametrically opposed to each other. (Newson in Malik 2012b)

Newson fails to offer an insight into what he wanted to achieve with the combination of choreography and spoken word within the scenes discussed, instead offering the justification that every word is 'real' and that the material was treated 'fairly' and 'accurately', perhaps implying in this response that his focus was on achieving a neutral translation. He suggests that it is unfair of Malik to be offended by his portrayal of characters as the words used are not his own, nor the company's but those of the interviewees.

Newson's response to Malik's assertion that the production had too narrow a viewpoint and did not reflect on what this was, perhaps exposing Newson's at least partial understanding of the verbatim theatre practitioner's role as that of neutral and fair translator.

The ambition of the show, and its willingness to stomp all over the debate, is its great strength; its unwillingness to be more nuanced about whose boots are stomping where is its great weakness (Malik 2012a).

> I would argue it is Kenan who has missed many of the nuances in the work and on one level I appreciate why. It is a compact and dense work – one viewing is hardly enough to hear and digest all of the details presented. A number of people have come back to see the production more than once, and inevitably say they have understood and learned much more from a second viewing. However, I take exception to the allegation that the production 'stomps all over the debate' in such an apparently clumsy fashion. The development of *Can We Talk About This?* involved over a year of research by myself and the DV8 team and has been refined over another 12 months of touring. Many of the interviewees in *Can We Talk About This?* are the world's leading exponents on the issues of Islam, multiculturalism and free speech. Unlike Kenan, I think many of the thoughts and arguments they/we present are in fact very nuanced. If we were obliged to present every detail of each person and their story/body of work in order for the production to be seen as valid, I'm afraid we'd all still be sitting in the theatre watching the show. (Newson in Malik 2012b)

By not acknowledging that a verbatim piece of theatre will include the perceptions, reactions and opinions of those involved in creating it, Newson appears not to understand what Malik is calling for here. His response is to argue that he and the company took the time and effort to make sure they were well researched and did not 'misrepresent' any information, rather than acknowledging that this production, like any verbatim piece, is one specific version of events and characters and that the piece could have developed and focused on finding ways to highlight this within the performance itself.

Some of these verbatim practitioners' reflections on their work and process reveal some focus on creating 'raw', and to continue the food analogy, unprocessed performances. Scholarly engagement within performance discourse may be starting to shift the focus to include an understanding of verbatim material as unstable, multi-layered, acknowledging that the practitioners' geographic, cultural, political and personal positioning may elicit different performance material (Brown 2010; Forsyth and Megson 2009; Martin 2013; Radosavljevic 2013). However, many verbatim theatre practitioners are perhaps still locked in an understanding of their role as neutral translators, carefully transferring meaning from interview to stage.

In order to deepen and extend the 'dialogized heteroglossia' in which DV8's movement translations of the verbatim material challenge, confront, parody and collide with their source text the verbatim theatre practitioner must Newson find explicit ways to accept, locate, acknowledge, expose and play with his own editorial choices and agency in verbatim performance material? In order to understand the shift in perception of the role of a verbatim theatre practitioner it is productive to consider two previous dialogues and transformations in thinking within documentary film studies and translation studies. Both fields have questioned whether the focus on authenticity, fidelity, equivalence and neutrality needs to be shifted in order for the practice to allow more creativity and move forward. The analysis of verbatim theatre could benefit by borrowing from discourses in many different disciplines, including cultural studies, languages and linguistics, media and communication studies, reception studies, performance studies, documentary film studies and translation studies. It is useful to examine how understanding of the role of the documentary film maker and translator has developed and how these practitioners have sought ways to explicitly acknowledge the existence of their own agency, perceptions and positions in their work in order to find ways for the 'self' to encounter the 'other' in a meaningful negotiation and discourse. Bakhtin (1981) cited both the inclusion of voices from different members of society, including 'ordinary people', and the use of different languages (and a physical language, in the case of the clown) as examples of 'dialogized heteroglossia'. Verbatim theatre's relationship to documentary film lies in the collection and inclusion of many different individuals from society and the relation to translation lies in the process of translating the spoken words into movement. Similar to the role of a documentary film-maker, the first stage of the verbatim theatre process is the research, collecting, editing and putting together of a 'documentary' script, whether that is an audio script as in the case of DV8 and Recorded Delivery or a transcribed script as in the case of Soans. The second stage of the process is translating that script into live performance. Before exploring the changing perception of the role of the translator, the focus of this chapter, it is useful to briefly address how the perceived role of the documentary film-maker has shifted from a belief in the possibility of being an objective film-maker to one of being a reflexive film-maker.

Documentary Film and Actuality

> Less than at any time does the simple reproduction of reality tell us anything about reality... Therefore something has actually to be constructed, something artificial, something set up. (Brecht, cited in Benjamin 1931: 24)

Brecht's theories of performance practice were influenced by his understanding of film-maker Eisenstein's theory of montage. Documentary film theorists drew on Brecht's theories of reflexive performance to influence documentary film practice. Now can an understanding of documentary film discourse influence verbatim theatre theory and practice and challenge the anti-theatrical culture? Actuality, fact, truth, reality, has been a constant issue in documentary history since the inception of cinema, culminating in the 1990s, when the issue was brought into specific focus. The question of what constitutes reality has been central to documentary film discourse since the advent of film. For instance, the Lumiére brothers' exhibition at the Grand Café in Paris in 1895, the first public screening of a documentary film, comprised 'both pre-documentary "actualities" and fiction based vignettes shown together without distinction' (Ellis and McLane 2005: 293). Aspects of the Lumiéres' footage, for example, the fact that the workers avoid looking at the camera when they are filmed leaving the factory, suggest that parts of the film were constructed or rehearsed. Already in 1895, therefore we find the 'dialect between the "real" and the "staged", which has continuously been included in discussion of documentary, was already in play' (ibid.).

Brecht was concerned with 'constructed' images that revealed the actuality of a situation, believing that something 'set up' could create a dialectical space that would 'expose the contradictions in social reality and depict society as an ever changing process' (Bradley 2006: 4). Brecht was influenced by Eisenstein's theory of montage which was centred on the idea of contradiction or conflict. Eisenstein argued that it was the construction, in his case the editing of images, that led to an understanding of reality and he believed that conflict was central to life and art, asserting that 'when two (or more) shots are juxtaposed, a meaning emerges from their collision that was not present in the separate shots' (Shaw 2008: 9). Both Brecht and Eisenstein believed that something had to be 'constructed' to allow contradictions to 'confront each other dialectically' (Benjamin [1931] 2003: 8), in order to tell us anything about reality. Since Brecht, a debate has arisen between those who believe in the possibility of positivistic objective film-making and Brechtian reflexive film-makers who believe that, in order to comment on reality, objects are necessarily constructed and that these aspects should be incorporated into the film and not concealed from view.

Those who disagree with Brecht and Eisenstein believe that documentary's tradition has been one of striving to achieve an objective representation of reality. Since its invention in the nineteenth century, 'photography was endowed with a transcendental, scientific capacity even as it adopted the idiom of art' (Lippit 1999: 68) and many believed the camera was a scientific tool that could record accurate evidence (Gunning 1999). This debate about whether documentary could or should represent an objective, unmediated reality came into sharp focus during the 1990s when it acquired a legal dimension. Winston (2008) points out that 'in the 1990s it became increasingly dangerous to be a documentary film-maker' (Winston 2008: 9). He argues that the documentary film-maker's freedom to work without censorship was under threat, stating that, 'for the first time legally backed sanctions were being invoked against any who pass off as real scenes those that had been in some way tampered with' (ibid.). Winston points to a significant body of people who believed it possible for a camera to be switched on and left alone to collect footage that represented the actual situation in which manipulation and bias had played no part (ibid.). In 1992, documentary film-maker Nick Broomfield's *The Leader, His Driver and the Driver's Wife* became the subject of the first ever libel action against Channel 4 taken to trial when Jani Allan, a woman referred to in the documentary, accused Channel 4 and Broomfield of depicting her as a 'woman of easy virtue' (The Independent 1992). This was not an isolated incident and there is now a heightened public and media awareness about misrepresentation of truth in documentary film, prompting some to react defensively. Alan Boyd, a producer for the BBC, defended the documentary genre in an interview for *The Guardian* newspaper by saying 'Documentary makers are not liars and they don't manipulate things', adding that any manipulation in documentary making was 'unacceptable', while Mark Thompson, director-general of the BBC, stated that the BBC must 'never deceive the public' (Jack 2007). This view that documentary must present an unadulterated reality raises important questions about actuality in documentary film-making.

The demand for observational purity ignored a variety of everyday procedures and choices, such as the very decision to make a film in the first instance through to choice of camera angle for each scene, all of which inevitably impact on the film being made. Film-makers seeking a faithful representation generally assumed that the production process must be masked, as evident in the case of direct cinema, in which technological advances allowed the use of lighter equipment to record reality with the least possible intervention. Bruzzi (2000) argues that the view of documentary's history as concerned with presenting an unmediated truth 'is only valid if one takes as representative of the documentary 'canon' films that seek to hide the modes of production' (Bruzzi 2000: 154). She points out that the historiography of documentary reveals the marginalisation of a more reflexive documentary tradition apparent in films such as *Man with a Movie Camera, A propos de Nice* and *Land Without Bread* (Bruzzi 2000: 154–155). Vertov, Vigo and Buñuel are among the film-makers who address the problematic notion that film can capture a single truth within their work.

Directly questioning the notion that film can present footage not 'tampered with' in any way, film theorists such as Renov (1993) suggest that attempts by documentary films to '"fix" on celluloid what lies before the camera - ourselves or members of other cultures - are fragile if not altogether insincere efforts' (Renov 1993: 26). Renov refers to a series of decisions, such as how shots are chosen in the edit, that result in the product being 'mediated, the result of multiple interventions that necessarily come between the cinematic sign (what we see on the screen) and its referent (what existed in the world)' (ibid.). Renov (1993) in his chapter '*Toward a Poetics of Documentary*' outlines four tendencies of documentary, 'To record, reveal, or preserve; To persuade or promote; To analyze or interrogate; To express'. Renov focuses on the range of different processes and devices utilised by film-makers in order to move away from an understanding that documentary film-makers should strive only to 'preserve' meaning. As well as challenging the assumption that preservation of meaning is important or even possible, he suggests that an open awareness of these four tendencies has the possibility to 'enrich' the creative practice of documentary film-making. Derrida, referring directly to television and the effect of tele-technologies on the philosophical and political climate of the 1990s, argues that 'actuality' is invariably a matter of 'artifactuality' involving a selection and editing process (Derrida and Stiegler 2002: 42). Contrasting Renov and Derrida's idea that all film is 'mediated' with the desire for an unaltered truth, presents documentary with a challenging contradiction, setting the positivistic belief in objectivity against the view that any reflection on society inevitably includes subjective perceptions, shaped by the perceiver's beliefs, attitudes, values and their historical context. Rabiger (2004) and Grierson (1966) suggest that this subjective representation is at the heart of documentary film and provides its purpose and power. Rabiger asserts that 'True documentary reflects the richness and ambiguity of life, and goes beyond the guise of objective observation to include impressions, perceptions and feelings' (Rabiger 2004: 108), while Grierson (1966) defined documentary as, 'the creative treatment of actuality'.

What Rabiger (2004) terms the 'technique of reflexivity' is a mode that makes no attempt to disguise, in fact emphasises, the production process in making a film. Vertov draws our attention to the camera in *Man with a Movie Camera*, by making the filming process visible. In Michael Moore's films the presence of his whole crew is evident. These are examples of reflexive film-makers who are not afraid to both make creative decisions to create interesting films and reveal these decisions. Rabiger suggests that these film-makers take issue with the view that the means of production should be hidden so as not to 'interfere' with reality, arguing that the collection of totally objective film footage is an unachievable utopian aim. Agreeing with Brecht, these film-makers believe that documentary should not simply try to reproduce reality but should highlight the complex notion of reality by making visible the different perspectives or actualities that inhabit the same film. Film-makers such as Moore and Broomfield, who often appear in their own films as central characters, seek to highlight the production process, resulting in films where actuality or meaning can be found in the negotiation between film-maker, subjects and audience. Whereas for several film-makers this reflexive approach is used as an occasional technique, Rabiger suggests that there is a shift needed in documentary film in which reflexivity informs every practitioners' entire style of film-making, with the ongoing dialogue between film-maker, subject and audience creating the space that enables subtle and unusual readings as the audience find their own meaning.

Translation: Creativity and Agency

As discussed in Chapter 1, discussions surrounding fidelity, equivalence and neutrality have been central to translation studies. The apparent hegemonic consideration of 'authenticity' and 'respect' in verbatim theatre has perhaps lead to Edgar's quip which light-heartedly suggests an absence of creativity in the theatrical movement. Edgar's quip resonates with translation scholar Robinson's (1998: 92) belief that translation's long history of focusing on errors and textual equivalence has resulted in translators with 'a chronic unwillingness to take risks'. In the same way as the call for a shift in documentary practice and Rabiger's undermining of the concept of objective observation and his call for practitioners to be aware that their films will and should 'include impressions, perceptions and feelings' (Rabiger 2004: 108), translation theorists have undermined the concept of fidelity, equivalence and neutrality.

In translation studies there is a significant history of friction between translation scholars who believe 'creativity' is something that cannot be separated from a translator's practice and those that observe that it is something that goes beyond the parameters of a translator's role (O'Sullivan 2013). The definition of 'creativity' in relation to translation practice has varied from scholar to scholar, but as O'Sullivan (2013: 43) notes, it is the focus on the translator's personal decisions and deviations from a 'word-for-word' translation that is often viewed as the creative practice. O'Sullivan (2013: 42) notes that 'references to creativity tend to presuppose the existence of a, *tertium comparationis* a literal translation against which non-literal translation strategies can be labelled as creative'. The very possibility of the existence of a *tertium comparationis* is complicated and challenged by postmodern critical theory, and resonates with Bakhtin's assertions that monoglossic writing that presented a single-voiced discourse failed to acknowledge the inherent heteroglossia present in all aspects of life. Thus, just as Perteghella (2013) suggests that the processes of creative writing and translation cannot be detached from each other, I would argue that every translation of verbatim material into live performance involves a degree of creative and subjective practice. Perteghella (2013) asserts that within any translation, the translator's subjectivity will always be present and depending on presentation of the translation 'will become more or less visible'. How a verbatim theatre practitioner chooses to place the material onto the presentational space will offer the audience a different reading. Every choice of movement, spacing, costume, vocal performance and performance space has been chosen by one or a team of theatre/dance practitioners and is therefore a creative choice. Perhaps then the important question, from the perspective of a theatre practitioner, is not whether a focus on the role of a 'neutral translator' is stifling theatrical creativity, but how the creative choices and subjective process can become more visible? O'Sullivan (2013: 46) suggests that translators' training would benefit from a stronger focus on divergent and creative thinking and practice and postulates that creativity 'is something which happens in translations and is demanded of translators'.

The literary translation envisaged here advocates translation not solely as a linguistic skill and/or a powerful cultural practice, but essentially as a creative writing practice, shapeshifting, moving around borders, working with materials and materiality, travelling through genres, zooming in at the process itself and at the translator's subjectivity marked and visible within the 'new' text and in the different drafts this subjectivity produces (Perteghella 2013).

Tymoczko, in her article 'Reconceptualising Translation Theory: Integrating Non-Western Thought about Translation' (2005) and in her book *Enlarging Translation; Empowering Translators* (2007), asserts that translation studies needs to enlarge its boundaries and enable translators to work in a way that rejects the idea and concept of 'empirical meaning' as something that is pinpointed and accurately 'carried across' from source to target text. She suggests that this shift in thinking will 'shake the foundations of translation theory and practice as they are known at present' (2005: 1083) 'thus liberating their translation practices from the false dictate to preserve meaning' (2007: 265). Translation theorists have attempted to empower translators to practice with an increased understanding that a translation, like any reading of a text, unearths diverse responses depending on the translator (Batchelor 2008; Pym 2010; Tymoczko 2007; Wolf 2008). Tymoczko explains her understanding of meaning and language as unstable and evolutionary by affirming that '[a] text elicits different responses depending on the individual reader's (or hearer's) experience, situated knowledge, and affective life, and the meaning of the text is configured differently as a result' (2007: 285).

This understanding of a translation, that it is a conversation or negotiation between source text and translator, resonates with Rabiger's position that documentary film places the film's material and subject in dialogue with film-maker's beliefs, attitudes, values and their geographical, social and historical context. Similar to Rabiger's (2004) description of the 'technique of reflexivity' as a mode in which film-makers reveal and emphasise the production decisions and process in making a film in order to stress the films subjective status, Tymoczko (2007) calls for translations to foreground the agency of the translator. Tymoczko suggests that this shift in thinking about the conceptualisation of translation has the most significant impact on the role of the translator. In her article 'Why Translators Should Want to Internationalize Translation Studies' (2009), she asserts that this distancing from a Eurocentric definition of translation and its 'false dictate' that a translator's role is to find an equivalence with a focus on neutrality 'offers new models of practice, greater potential for creativity, enhancement of the translator's agency, new ethical positioning, the ability to assess translational phenomena with greater acuity, and a reservoir of conceptualizations for meeting challenges of the present and the future' (2009: 401).

Tymoczko (2007: 82–100) subverts positivistic lines of reasoning and suggests that translation should be viewed as a cluster concept with no exact definition, but rather taking meaning from many different world cultures and models for translation. There are of course many facets to Tymoczko's translation theory, but I am interested in exploring how Tymoczko applies her theory of how 'internationalizing' translation will allow 'new models of practice', thus resulting in 'greater potential for creativity' and 'enhancement of the translator's agency'. This chapter will later explore if an understanding of this discussion in translation studies can provide a framework for considering the shifting role of verbatim performance practitioners. Tymoczko gives examples of how the consideration of some 'cognitive metaphors' for translation from other cultures could offer new creative models of practice and ways of working for contemporary translators. She explains that 'China has practiced group translation for more than two thousand years' (2009: 410) and that some Buddhist sutra translation groups could involve thousands of people. She offers the example of the history of 'group translation methods' (Tymoczko 2009: 410) in China to challenge the Eurocentric view that translators work individually. Tymoczko demonstrates that the view of translation practices in both Africa and India 'stress the translator's role as narrator and they imply change and translational creativity' (2009: 407). She provides the example of the Igbo words tapia and kowa as terms for translation that incorporate the sense 'break it up and tell it (in a different form)' (Tymoczko 2007: 71). She also references words from various

Indian languages such as 'anuvad (literally 'following after'), rupantar ('change in form') and chaya ('shadow', used of very literal translations)' (Tymoczko 2007: 68–70). Tymoczko provides these examples of 'narrative models associated with translation practices in Africa, India and elsewhere' (2009: 410) to challenge the Eurocentric view that a translation cannot diverge significantly from the source text, pointing out that 'the cognitive metaphors of words for translation in these cultures acknowledge the necessity of breaking up the source text and reformulating it to adapt to the receiving audience' (2009: 410). Tymoczko also offers the example that in Arabic tradition the 'knowledge of the translator was expected to be equal to or greater than that of the author of the source text, again change and updating were expected in the translated product' (Tymoczko 2009: 410). Tymoczko offers this lens through which to view translation practice in order to challenge the Eurocentric view that translations cannot add new meaning to the source text. Tymoczko asserts that this consideration of the 'cognitive metaphors' for translation from different parts of the world provides an alternative to dominant models of translation practice, allowing translators to view their practice as open, allowing them to 'borrow, blend and invent new translation strategies' (Tymoczko 2009: 411). It is this recognition that translators need to be flexible, imaginative problem-solvers that Tymoczko believes will empower translators to be creative practitioners. Another important aspect in Tymoczko's proposed shake-up of the foundations of translation practice is the enhancement of the agency of translators. Tymoczko asserts that throughout Western Europe, due to a cultural concern to control meaning, 'the role of translators in making meaning has frequently been effaced in Eurocentric tradition' (2009: 412). Tymoczko urges translators to recognise the importance of their involvement in the creation of new meaning and to be 'active cultural agents'.

Verbatim Dance-Theatre in Conversation with Documentary Film Studies and Translation Studies

All verbatim theatre practice has included a focus on the collecting and playing or staging of the words of individuals. Anderson and Wilkinson (2007: 4) explain that the documentary/verbatim theatre work in the UK in 1960s 'provided a platform for the silent or marginalised in those communities', while Derbyshire and Hodson (2008: 13) suggest that verbatim theatre in the twenty-first century is 'giving voice to the point of view of the dispossessed'. By examining verbatim theatre practitioners commentary on their practice and placing this analysis in dialogue with pertinent concepts located in translation studies and documentary film studies, questions have arisen regarding if verbatim theatre might have an increased potential to offer people who are often marginalised and silenced by society a voice if the performance text includes an awareness of the agency of the choreographer/director/performers. Tymoczko (2007) calls for translations to foreground the agency and voice of the translator in order to become 'active cultural agents'. Can experimental practice with a focus on the body in performance find and enable devising processes that empower the practitioners to position themselves as 'active cultural agents' in order to find ways in which to foreground their choreographic voices? What devising and choreographic processes and exercises can be developed that enables ongoing dialogue between source material, choreographer, director, dancer and audience thus creating a space that facilitates subtle and unusual readings from an audience able to find their own meaning? Does the fact that the source material is being translated through and delivered alongside movement highlight the director/choreographer's role in the construction and presentation of the text? Is there potential to include performance material that exposes the editing and choreographic processes?

Tymoczko's critique and proposals for translation and Rabiger and Renov's for documentary are equally valid and particularly interesting when applied to verbatim theatre. Debates have surfaced in both of these fields that have considered the right to alter, edit, re-form and add new meaning to source material, thus making translators/film-makers 'active cultural agents' and 'enriching' the creative process. Problems are arising for verbatim theatre practitioners similar to those that theorists have identified in translation studies and documentary film studies. As discussed above, verbatim theatre can present itself as a precise/decisive/ complete investigation of an event/subject rather than highlighting its status as one specific or possible understanding/version/reading. Young (2009) identifies a clear parallel to the division in documentary film and television, between reflexive and objective approaches, in verbatim theatre. He describes a distinction between verbatim theatre that seeks to 'record' and verbatim theatre that seeks to 'report'. The former, he argues, aims for a representation of an objective reality by seeking 'to efface the creators and their subjectivity' (Young 2009: 72), while the latter 'recognizes that such facts and information are value-laden and acknowledges the documentary maker's place in the mode of production' (Young 2009: 72).

Gardner (2007) suggests that while critical response to documentary television has developed beyond the belief that the camera could present an unmediated truth, the same questions directed at documentary television now need to be applied to verbatim theatre, arguing that,

> It seems that whereas most of us are quite aware when we watch a reality TV show that what we're seeing is strongly shaped and filtered through an editing process, when we watch verbatim theatre we quickly lose sight of that mediation. The result? We accept what is presented to us as true without questioning how statements have been selected and organised. (Gardner 2007)

Bottoms (2006) argues that, in order to encourage the critical response described as necessary by Gardner, theatre practitioners should, like documentary film-makers, incorporate into their work the Brechtian belief that an audience should be constantly aware that they are watching an artificial and constructed situation (Finney 2006). Bottoms (2006) asserts that practitioners should un-mask their selection/production processes in an attempt to remind the audience that what they are watching is being mediated and that verbatim theatre which fails to do so 'can too easily become disingenuous exercises in the presentation of "truth," failing (or refusing?) to acknowledge their own highly selective manipulation of opinion and rhetoric' (Bottoms 2006: 57).

Young suggests that reflexive writing or staging techniques are not used by current British playwrights and directors, saying that 'self-reflexivity has been largely absent from the wave of documentary theatre that has swept Britain in the last few years' (Young 2009: 73). He argues that 'British plays and their productions tend to eschew all touches of theatricality, emphasizing above all the faithful representation of the words, vocal inflexions, and physical gestures of their interviewee-characters' (Young 2009: 72). Bottoms (2006) agrees and referring to the work of Hare and Soans, says 'the current "verbatim theatre" trend in London has tended to lionize plays that are both manipulative and worryingly unreflexive regarding the "realities" they purport to discuss' (Bottoms 2006: 57). Bottoms and Young argue that it is essential that verbatim theatre makers develop more creative techniques of representation in order to engage a critically active audience.

When transferring an audio recording of a story/experience/memory/conversation to a live performance there is a form of cultural negotiation anchored and enmeshed in discourses of identity, of self and other and structures of power. The methods by which a practitioner translates/transforms this recording into performance material emulate and expose the artists' conjectures, perspective and intentions. The fact that different directors/choreographers could start with the same audio recordings and create profoundly different live performances illustrates that, as with translation studies and documentary film studies, there needs to be a call for a significant shift in how we view the role of a verbatim theatre practitioner. What is interesting to consider is how this shift in perspective can be exploited to open-out and develop creative approaches to choreographing verbatim dance-theatre. With a focus on the creative treatment and appropriation of the verbatim material comes a renewed importance to find ways of exposing the director/choreographers intentions and assumptions within the performance itself. Within this consideration of the degree to which verbatim translations include political/cultural/personal appropriation of their source material one important question arises: Is there space for creative expression in a technique that positions itself as predicated on document and testimony?

Young and Bottoms' call for the development of reflexive verbatim theatre practice profoundly resonates with Batchelor (2008), Loffredo (2008), Perteghella (2008), Tymoczko (2005, 2007, 2009) and O'Sullivan's demand for creative translation practice that acknowledges and unveils the translator's subjective position and role in the translation, as well as the plea from Renov, Rabiger and Grierson's for a practice that is brave enough to reveal the complexity of personal perceptions and emotions involved in the film-making process. A consideration of the shift in thinking about the role of documentary film-makers and translators offers a rich framework within which the role of the verbatim theatre practitioner can be examined, unsettled and thus transformed. Returning to the discussion about heteroglossia in performance, I believe that experimenting by placing the verbatim interview material on stage together with its on stage movement translation, providing a double-voiced discourse between spoken/recorded language and movement, has the potential to prompt the viewer to consider the dialectic between the verbatim material and its onstage translation. The specific reflections on documentary film-makers' and translators' role as practitioners explored above have been selected to inform and deepen an understanding of how heteroglossic performance material might be produced in this way by focusing on creating and displaying multiple modes of communication within the performance material.

Renov (2003) in his chapter 'Toward a Poetics of Documentary' outlines four tendencies of documentary, 'To record, reveal, or preserve; To persuade or promote; To analyze or interrogate; To express'. A consideration of each of these tendencies in relation to verbatim theatre can help expand an understanding of the role of verbatim theatre practitioner and how verbatim dance-theatre incorporates these four characteristics. An exploration of Renov's techniques has unearthed some possible approaches to creating and structuring a double-voiced on stage translation containing the potential to produce performance material which highlights that the production is not the carrier, or conveyer, of meaning but rather the provocation of meaning.

An examination of how Tymoczko challenges the accepted role of the translator offers exciting possibilities for how we can view the role of verbatim performance practitioner and how a choreographic translation of recorded/spoken language can be approached. There are of course many facets to Tymoczko's translation theory, but it is Tymoczko's opening out of the understanding of the role of the translator in order to allow 'new models of practice' resulting in 'greater potential for creativity' and 'enhancement of the translator's agency' that is relevant and which I will attempt to apply to verbatim performance. Can an understanding of this discussion in translation studies provide a useful framework for considering the shifting role of verbatim performance practitioners?

A central problem relating to understanding the verbatim practitioner's role is the reliance on the concept of a single truth which can result in verbatim theatre directors rejecting a collaborative approach with their cast and discarding creative and theatrical approaches to creating work which results in the restrictive aim of locating and carrying across meaning without any manipulation. Blythe and Newson have attempted to broaden the boundaries of verbatim performance by working across and between disciplines whether that is theatre and music or theatre and dance. I would suggest that it is through this interdisciplinary approach, particularly dance-theatre, that verbatim performance will continue to evolve and present engaging performance work.

Tymoczko explores examples of how taking account of 'cognitive metaphors' for translation from other cultures could offer new creative models of practice and ways of working for contemporary translators.

There are a few of Tymoczko's specific examples of the opening-out of the understanding of the role of a translation/role of a translator that resonate with the discussion about verbatim performance and which offer an excellent starting point for considering new models of practice in verbatim performance that allow 'greater potential for creativity'. Renov's argument that 'attempts to "fix" on celluloid what lies before the camera - ourselves or members of other cultures - are fragile if not altogether insincere efforts' can be applied as a reminder to verbatim theatre practitioners that all verbatim theatre performances are the result of many choices and are therefore undeniably mediated works. This can challenge the concept of fidelity and the belief that a verbatim theatre practitioner's role is to record and preserve meaning and can help shift an definition of the role to that of finding ways of staging that are different to these 'fragile' and unstable attempts.

Rather than accepting the phenomenon of static performers delivering 'faithful' verbatim dialogue in an attempt to collapse the gap between the 'reality' and the performance, it is instructive to consider ways in which verbatim dance-theatre can instead find ways to broaden that gap by rejecting the emphasis on placing the audience in the role of interviewer and highlighting the processes of manipulation. Two important features already explored by dance-theatre choreographers are repetition and discontinuity, which can be used in verbatim theatre to expand this gap and make it visible to an audience. For example: The same words could be spoken by the same performer with two very different movement phrases; or the same movement phrase could accompany a differently edited version of the words; or the same words could be spoken and the same movement phrase performed by a different performer; or a performer could deliver an edited version of the words and then the audio track could play a different edited version of the words. These few examples of the many possible uses of repetition suggest the ways in which its use could be utilised to reveal the editor's/choreographer's/performer's choices. The use of repetition could also be developed to include responses to the same material by different individual performers and/or choreographers. As discussed above, Tymoczko (**2009**: 410) offers the example of the history of 'group translation methods' in China to challenge the Eurocentric view that translators work individually. Rather than focusing on a single-author/director/choreographer it would be interesting to view what possibilities arise when collaborative devised processes are applied to creating verbatim theatre. What layers are added when choreographer and performers work together to respond to and negotiate their response to verbatim material? What creative processes can be developed to allow for these different responses to emerge and enter into a dialogue with each other in performance? Renov's assertion that the use of 'interviews, evocative images, and statistical information' (2003: 26) are all devices to persuade or promote serves to emphasise the importance for verbatim theatre practitioners to be aware that their piece of work is the result of a specific constructed situation and created with certain intentions. Applying this concept to an understanding of the role of verbatim theatre practitioner directly challenges the concept of neutrality and unsettles the understanding of this role as a neutral carrier of collected material to performance. Therefore what becomes important is for a practitioner to find ways in which to make explicit the many intentions that may be present.

Tymoczko (2007: 71) offers the example of the Igbo words *tapia* and *kowa* as terms for translation that incorporate the sense of fracturing and transformation, an understanding that a translation will 'break it up and tell it (in a different form)'. What possibilities are there for verbatim performance to break apart the collected material into multiple pieces and re-form the material with a focus on making new connections in creative and exciting ways? Renov understands that in order to encourage an audience to actively 'analyze and even act upon what it sees' (2003: 27) a film-maker needs to disturb the direct connection between the film and the 'reality', provides a way to think about approaching the 'fracturing' of the performance text. He suggests that one way to achieve this is 'to call attention to the complementary relationship between sound and image' (ibid.), suggesting that a voice-over of a documentary providing a cynical or judgemental view of the images presented would draw the audience's attention to the fact they were watching an interpretation of something and therefore encourage their own analysis or interrogation of what they were viewing. Applying this concept to verbatim theatre challenges the concept of equivalence and facilitates an understanding of the role of verbatim theatre practitioner as moving away from trying to replicate something to analysing and investigating something. The presentation of the spoken/recorded language of the verbatim interview and its movement translation can offer creative ways in which to disrupt the complementary relationship between the verbatim words spoken and the movement performed. Complex uses of choreography can either support and extend or diverge from and assault the rhythm/tone/meaning/

relationships involved in the words. This double-voiced discourse has the potential to produce a distinct gap between the audio and visual aspects of the performance, and within that gap the audience can begin to analyse and interrogate the performance material.

Tymoczko's example of the understanding within the Arabic tradition that a translator should add new meaning during the translation process challenges the Eurocentric view that translations cannot alter the meaning of the source text and raises the possibility for a performance text to highlight what it is adding and therefore how it is different to the verbatim text. This understanding could help shift verbatim performance practitioners from focusing on a 'faithful' translation to the view that a piece of verbatim performance should do more than offer the audience a glimpse of the collected material by adding new meaning. In what ways can verbatim performance add new meaning by exploring a physical response to the collected material and presenting this as a double-voiced discourse? In similar vein, Renov suggests that the majority of representations of reality are 'more functional than artistic' in their attempt to appear objective, arguing that it is important to make engaging work and use creativity and personal expression again to unveil this gap between 'reality' and representation, which is best achieved by 'denaturalizing the image'. Dance-theatre, with its emphasis on physical expression, demands the creative exploration of what the body can express and communicate. Dance-theatre can reject both the linear narratives and clearly defined character of Western Classical dance and the abstract movement of formalist modern/postmodern dance. Within the realm of verbatim theatre, dance-theatre productions could experiment with making visible the struggle, sweat, focus and resolution to find numerous combinations of ways in which to excavate, illuminate and/or add to what is expressed in the spoken or recorded interviews. Rather than trying to emulate the seen or imagined natural body language of the people whose words they are presenting, choreographed movement can take part in a visible confrontation and dialogue with the verbatim material.

The significant shift in interpretation of the role of documentary film-maker as someone who can include 'impressions, perceptions and feelings' to create films enabling an ongoing dialogue between film-maker, subject and audience, relies on the 'technique of reflexivity' which is rooted in Brechtian Theatre. At one level the influence of this concept on verbatim theatre is obvious, in the use of reflexive techniques as developed by Brechtian theatre (performers move between characters, direct questions at the audience, interact with objects in a non-realistic set) which encourage an audience to remain aware of the theatre maker's role and position. Dance-theatre, which owes much to Brechtian theatre, also offers the possibility to extend this 'technique of reflexivity'. The creation of dance-theatre utilises the process of physical improvisation and this can be applied to verbatim theatre in which the choreographer or performer finds material through improvisational tasks, during which they provide an instant physical response whilst listening to collected recorded material. These individual improvisations, in which the mover instantly responds to material will of course include personal 'impressions, perceptions and feelings'. One way to potentially extend this 'technique of reflexivity' could be to stage live moments of improvisations in which a performer and the audience listen to recorded material, while the performer improvises. An extension of this would be to watch as the performer selects moments that make up a movement phrase which is then performed to an edited version of the audio recording, placing the choreographic devices in front of an audience and highlighting the performers' role in the appropriation of the material.

Verbatim theatre practitioners commentary on their creative process is often framed in terms of accuracy and fidelity. The inclusion of choreographic material or the development of verbatim dance-theatre may offer possible ways for verbatim theatre practitioners to move away from a process that includes questions such as 'Have we remained faithful to the interview material?' or 'Is this an accurate portrayal of the material?'. Even when working with choreographic material, is it only an explicit rejection of the understanding of a verbatim theatre practitioner as a neutral translator that will allow practitioners to intentionally explore the creation of performance material that acknowledges the gaps between the collected verbatim material and the final performance material.

References

Anderson, M., & Wilkinson, L. (2007). A Resurgence of Verbatim Theatre: Authenticity, Empathy and Transformation. *Australasian Drama Studies, 50*, 153–169.

Bakhtin, M. (1981). Discourse in the Novel (translated from Russian by M. Holquist and C. Emerson). In M. Holquist (Ed.), *The Dialogic Imagination* (pp. 259–422). Austin: University of Texas Press.

Batchelor, K. (2008). Third Spaces, Mimicry and Attention to Ambivalence: Applying Bhabhian Discourse to Translation Theory. *The Translator*, *14*(1), 51–70.
Benjamin, W. ([1931] 1972). A Short History of Photography. *Screen*, *13*(1), 5–26.
Bottoms, S. (2006). Putting the Document into Documentary: An Unwelcome Corrective? *The Drama Review*, *50*(3), 56–68.
Bradley, L. (2006). *Brecht and Political Theatre*. Oxford: Oxford University Press.
Brown, P. (Ed.). (2010). *Verbatim Theatre: Staging Memory and Community*. Sydney: Currency Press.
Bruzzi, S. (2000). *New Documentary: A Critical Introduction*. London: Routledge.
Derbyshire, H., & Hodson, L. (2008). Performing Injustice: Human Rights and Verbatim Theatre. *Law and Humanities* [online]. Available at: http://gala.gre.ac.uk/1450. Accessed 15 Apr 2012.
Derrida, J., & Stiegler, B. (2002). Echographies of Television: Filmed Interviews (translated from French by J. Bajarek). Cambridge: Polity Press.
Edgar, D. (2008). Doc and Dram. *The Guardian* [online]. Available at: https://www.theguardian.com/stage/2008/sep/27/theatre.davidedgar. Accessed 8 May 2010.
Ellis, J., & McLane, B. (2005). *A New History of Documentary Film*. London: Continuum International.
Finney, G. (2006). *Visual Culture in Twentieth-Century Germany: Text as Spectacle*. Bloomington, IN: Indiana University Press.
Forsyth, A., & Megson, C. (Eds.). (2009). *Get Real: Documentary Theatre Past and Present*. Basingstoke: Palgrave Macmillan.
Gardner, L. (2005). The Arab-Israeli Cookbook: Tricycle, London. *The Guardian* [online]. Available at: http://www.theguardian.com/stage/2005/jul/13/theatre. Accessed 24 Apr 2011.
Gardner, L. (2007). Does Verbatim Theatre Still Talk the Talk? *The Guardian* [online]. Available at: http://www.guardian.co.uk/stage/theatreblog/2007/may/07/foreditorsdoesverbatimthea. Accessed 8 May 2010.
Grierson, J. (1966). *Grierson on Documentary*. London: Faber.
Gunning, T. (1999). Embarrassing Evidence: The Detective Camera and the Documentary Impulse. In J. M. Gaines & M. Renov (Eds.), *Collecting Visible Evidence* (pp. 46–64). Minneapolis: University of Minnesota Press.
Hammond, W., & Steward, D. (Eds.). (2008). *Verbatim Verbatim: Techniques in Contemporary Documentary Theatre*. London: Oberon Books.
Hervey, S., Higgins, I., & Haywood, L. M. (1995). *Thinking Spanish Translation*. London: Routledge.
Jack, I. (2007). The Documentary Has Always Been a Confection Based on Lies. *The Guardian* [online]. Available at: http://www.guardian.co.uk/media/2007/jul/21/broadcastingethics.bbc. Accessed 2 Dec 2009.

Lane, D. (2010). *Contemporary British Drama*. Edinburgh: Edinburgh University Press.
Lippit, A. M. (1999). Phenomenologies of the Surface: Radiation-Body-Image. In J. M. Gaines & M. Renov (Eds.), *Collecting Visible Evidence* (pp. 65–83). Minneapolis: University of Minnesota Press.
Loffredo, E., & Perteghella, M. (Eds.). (2008). *One Poem in Search of a Translator: Rewriting 'Les Fenetres' by Apollinaire*. Bern: Peter Lang.
Malik, K. (2012a). We Should Talk About This. *Pandaemonium* [online]. Available at: https://kenanmalik.wordpress.com/2012/03/18/we-should-talk-about-this/. Accessed 12 Dec 2012.
Malik, K. (2012b). Lloyd Newson in Defence of 'Can We Talk About This?' *Pandaemonium* [online]. Available at: https://kenanmalik.wordpress.com/2012/05/28/lloyd-newson/. Accessed 12 Dec 2012.
Martin, C. (2013). *Theatre of the Real*. Basingstoke. Palgrave Macmillan.
Newmark, P. (1988). *A Textbook for Translation*. London: Prentice-Hall.
Niba, E. A., & Taber, C. R. (1966). *The Theory and Practice of Translation*. Leiden: Brill Archive.
O'Sullivan, C. (2012). Playing With(out) the Dictionary: Using Constrained Literature in the Development of Transferable Skills for Translators. *The Interpreter and Translator Trainer, 6*(2), 237–263.
O'Sullivan, C. (2013). Creativity. In *Handbook of Translation Studies* (Vol. 4, pp. 42–46). Amsterdam/Philadelphia, PA: John Benjamins.
Perteghella, M. (2008). Adaptation: Bastard Child or Critique? Putting Terminology Centre-Stage. *Journal of Romance Studies, 8*(3), 51–65.
Perteghella, M. (2013). Notes on the Art of Text Making. *The Creative Literary Studio* [Blog]. Available at: https://thecreativeliterarystudio.wordpress.com/tag/manuela-perteghella/. Accessed 6 Jan 2014.
Pym, A. (2010). *Exploring Translation Theories*. Abingdon: Routledge.
Rabiger, M. (2004). *Directing the Documentary* (4th ed.). Amsterdam: Elsevier.
Radosavljevi, D. (2013). *Theatre-Making: Interplay Between Text and Performance in the 21st Century*. Basingstoke: Palgrave Macmillan.
Renov, M. (1993). Toward a Poetics of Documentary. In M. Renov (Ed.), *Theorising Documentary* (pp. 12–36). London: Routledge.
Robinson, D. (1998). 22 Theses on Translation. *Journal of Translation Studies, 2*(6), 92–117.
Shaw, D. (2008). *Film and Philosophy: Taking Movies Seriously*. London: Wallflower.
Slovo, G. (2006, July 13). *Symposium on Verbatim Theatre Practices in Contemporary Theatre*.
The Independent. (1992). Journalist Denies Sex with Neo-Nazi. *The Independent* [online]. Available at: https://www.independent.co.uk/news/uk/journalist-denies-sex-with-neo-nazi-1534674.html. Accessed 2 Dec 2017.

Tymoczko, M. (2005). Reconceptualising Translation Theory: Integrating Non-Western Thought About Translation. In T. Hermans (Ed.), *Translating Others* (pp. 13–32). Manchester: St Jerome Publishing.

Tymoczko, M. (2007). *Enlarging Translation, Empowering Translators*. Manchester: St Jerome Publishing.

Tymoczko, M. (2009). Why Translators Should Want to Internationalize Translation Studies. *The Translator, 15*(2), 401–421.

Vinay, J. P., & Darbelnet, J. (1958). A Methodology for Translation (translated by Juan C. Sager & M. J. Hamel). In L. Venuti (Ed.), *The Translation Studies Reader* (pp. 84–93). London: Routledge.

Winston, B. (2008). *Claiming the Real II: Documentary: Grierson and Beyond*. Basingstoke: Palgrave Macmillan.

Wolf, M. (2008). Interference from the *Third Space*? The Construction of Cultural Identity Through Translation. In M. Muñoz-Calvo, C. Buesa-Gómez, & M. A. Ruiz-Moneva (Eds.), *New Trends in Translation and Cultural Identity* (pp. 11–20). Newcastle upon Tyne: Cambridge Scholars Publishing.

Young, S. (2009). Playing with Documentary Theatre: Aalstand Taking Care of Baby. *New Theatre Quarterly, 25*, 72–87.

CHAPTER 3

DV8 Physical Theatre's Verbatim Dance-Theatre: How Might Choreography Be Developed in Verbatim Performance?

Abstract Following Lloyd Newson's (DV8's To Be Straight With You: Dancing Against Prejudice, 2008) question, 'How do you combine stylized movement with verbatim text?', McCormack offers a detailed examination of some possible approaches to choreography developed in verbatim performance. The chapter considers the choreographic work of DV8 Physical Theatre, specifically their verbatim dance-theatre works *To Be Straight With You* (2007–2009) and *Can We Talk About This* (2011–2012). This chapter concludes with a consideration of if DV8 Physical Theatre's performance material highlights the complexity and instability of meaning, both in the source text (the verbatim interview material) and in the translation (the movement), by staging them side-by-side in a complex relationship to each other.

Keywords DV8 Physical Theatre · Choreography · Verbatim dance-theatre · Improvisation

Can concepts and ideas located in translation studies be engaged as a frame within which to examine the stage of choreographic process during which movement material is created in response to recorded spoken language in the form of a physical translation?

In 2008, Lloyd Newson, Artistic Director of DV8 Physical Theatre, asked 'How do you combine stylized movement with verbatim text?'.

For Newson, the constant commitment to push at and cross boundaries, what he describes as 'taking risks', is more important than any other aspect of choreography or performance making. Newson's career has been characterised by risk taking in a broad sense, whether that relates to experimenting with who a professional dancer can be; how far dancers can push their body before the movement becomes physically dangerous; whether dance can approach and generate complicated emotional narrative; or whether dance can engage with and contribute to important current issues and political debates. When asked about his thoughts on success in 1993, by which time DV8 had produced 11 performance projects and won numerous awards, Newson responded by explaining that his understanding of success centred wholly around the concept of 'pushing' the work.

When people refer to DV8 as a "successful" company, I question what they mean, what they define as successful. Just because a work is popular does not mean for me it is successful. Just because audiences like it doesn't mean it's good. Again success should be seen as a relative term. I believe that providing I keep pushing myself and do not rely on formula, I am successful (Newson 1993).

The fact that Newson says 'I only create when I have something to say' and that his approach to choreography is one of constant innovation, never developing a personal formula, has meant that the majority of published reflections on his work focus predominately on the subject matter explored by his work, his beliefs about what dance performance should achieve and the finished performance material itself. His focus is more on creating choreographic tasks and a creative space that produces material appropriate to the subject matter and therefore he has often been resistant or vague when discussing his choreographic practice.

DV8's Changing Relationship to Verbal Language

London-based DV8 Physical Theatre was initially founded in 1986 and since its formation has been led by Artistic Director Lloyd Newson. Originally conceived as a company aiming to confront what dance performance 'can and should address' (DV8 Physical Theatre 2018), DV8 was the first UK-based dance company to extend the work of the Ausdruckstanz and then *Tanztheater* genres to combine choreographed movement, pedestrian movement, recorded/spoken language, moving image, music, props and set to enlarge the expressive possibilities of a dance performance.

From the company's inception, a significant aspect of their work was to experiment with movement's relationship to spoken language in order to establish a choreographic approach that could tackle complex subject matter. The company's work sought to undo the work of Cunningham, Nikolais and other formalist choreographers who had fervently distanced dance from the world of theatre, acting or representation, in order to establish dance as a form of pure movement independent from symbols, psychology, representation, narrative or subject. Inspired by the work of Pina Bausch and the Tanztheater Wuppertal, DV8 were impelled to confront the damaging bifurcations between dance and meaning and to continue restoring dance-theatre as a discipline able to choreograph personal and political (non-linear) narrative. A decade on from Bausch's initial groundbreaking interdisciplinary choreographic work, DV8 introduced themselves as a UK-based company committed to working with all available forms, resisting the constraints of situating themselves within the boundaries of any restricted definitions of dance or theatre. Throughout his career, Newson has stressed the importance of the fact that DV8 works with trained dancers and that movement is the most important element of his storytelling technique, but while the primary focus is on movement, the company's work has developed a significant relationship with spoken/recorded language as well as using music or video/projection where appropriate.

> We find movement to express the meaning or idea we're presenting moment by moment, and if movement can't do it and words or song can, then we'll use those. Most dance companies, I feel, have restricted what they can speak about because they have accepted a limited definition of what movement constitutes 'dance'. (Newson 1998)

As well as extending and pushing the boundaries of what type of movement can be included in a dance performance, DV8 also experimented with what mediums could be combined with movement to create an engaging theatrical language. The company's entire body of work from 1985 to date demonstrates a commitment to the creative treatment and opening out of the possibilities of the relationship between recorded/spoken language and movement in performance. Just as Bausch's choreographic work extended the use of spoken word in dance performances such as Mary Wigman's *Totenmal* (1930), Martha Graham's *Deaths and Entrances* (1943) and Anna Teresa de Keersmaeker's *Elena's Aria*

(1984), with performers directly addressing the audience and blurring the lines between fictional and personal improvised language, DV8's work similarly moved language and movement into a much closer and more complex relationship. The experimentation with the relationship between recorded/spoken language and movement has shifted and evolved from project to project but the desire to explore the intricate, complex and specific possibilities of movement in relation to the similar complexities of spoken language is present in all of DV8's performance projects.

A central focus of DV8's redefinition of dance has been to change the relationship between choreographer and dancer, acknowledging that every dancer is a thinking, feeling person with a 'lived body' full of personal experience. Newson describes this concern as a reaction against his own professional experience of working as a dancer for choreographers who viewed their dancers as 'nothing more than a bit of pigment for them to paint with' (Newson 1992). DV8's work demonstrates a strong desire to enable the individual dancers to contribute to the creative process and draw on their individual differences, interests and skills. In what could be seen as an extension of Bausch's work, much of DV8's early work (*Bein' A Part, Lonely Art* (1985), *My Sex Our Dance* (1986), *Deep End* (1987), *Elemen T(h)ree Sex* (1987), *My Body, Your Body* (1987), *If Only* (1990)) was concerned with staging personal politics and performers drew on introspective structured improvisations to develop movement and spoken language to tackle subjects about complex human relationships such as isolation, loneliness, desire, trust or the pursuit of fulfilment. Improvisations in the studio saw Newson and the performers questioning, exploring and challenging themselves and the work created to make a connection with wider political or social debates through an acutely personal investigation in performance. These improvisations often placed the performers in an exposing and vulnerable position and Newson (1992) suggests that this sense of exposure could sometimes be the central concern of an improvisational task.

In one improvisational task reminiscent of a scene in Bausch's *Kontakthof* (2010), the performers walk forwards towards the audience and individually present themselves and different parts of their body, followed by contorted movement that suggests the repositioning and or hiding of parts of themselves. This offers possible readings of slave-show, prostitution, exposing relationships, stage performances, medical examinations and criminal trials. Newson explains that 'I often set tasks that ask performers to reveal something of their inner selves that they may not want to show in public' (Newson 1992). Newson also exposed parts of himself to inform the creation of movement, for example, in the creation process for *Strange Fish* (1992) Newson shared the experience of waking up with someone's arm on his body and asking the question 'is this trapped, or is this embraced?' to inform an improvisation that asked his performers to experiment and find ways, through movement and spoken language, to explore the entwined existence of intimacy and entrapment (Newson 1992). This improvisation developed some of the material for the intimate duet performed by Lauren Potter and Jordi Cortes Molin, in which they have their hands tightly clasped throughout. Whilst reflecting on the creation process for *Strange Fish* and his previous work, Newson describes a feeling of exhaustion arising from the way the company focused wholly inwards in order to create work. 'The way we'd done things was so personal and direct that we needed to find a more stylistic approach that could make us enjoy creating again' (Newson 1992).

It is in this departure from the 'personal' that Newson began to explore the relationship of movement to recorded/spoken language in a way that pushed past Bausch and his contemporaries' experimentation and presentation of the same relationship. In 1993, DV8 embarked on the performance project *MSM* (1993) that endeavoured to 'extend DV8's use of language and its relationship to movement' (DV8 1993) and for the first time the company collected and transcribed interview material to use as a starting point for a piece of choreography. The collected material aimed to investigate male sexuality outside the parameters of society. The title of the piece is a term located in Sociology used to refer to men who have sex with men in public toilets and Newson and the performers collected interviews with '50 men of different ages, backgrounds and sexualities, investigating their desires, fantasies and realities' (DV8 1993). The creation process for *MSM* followed a similar process of generating material through improvisation with Newson then selecting, developing and choreographing the material into a highly structured piece of performance. However, rather than improvisations that required the performers to respond to Newson's or their own personal experience, improvisations were set up to illuminate and analyse the verbatim material.

The use of verbatim material as the starting point meant that the company played with and created new devising processes that focused on illuminating and expressing the words located in the interview. The central aim of improvisations in the creation process shifted significantly from the co-creation of words and movement based on personal introspection to the creation of movement material that will illuminate, add layers and find ways to express the emotional, physical or sensual aspects of the interview not communicated through the recorded words. Perhaps Newson believed that he had exhausted the choreographic possibilities of exploring male sexuality in his previous body of work through improvisation alone and this new technique of choreographing as a response to a script pieced together from verbatim material would offer a fresh way of exploring the same subject. This new technique did result in new and different choreographic material that had a much clearer focus on the relationship between spoken language and movement than on the movement itself. In pieces such as *Strange Fish* (1992) and *Dead Dreams of Monochrome Men* (1988), spoken language appeared at times but more often than not those words would then be left to resonate through the body and extensive movement sequences. However, in *MSM* there was a constant connection between movement and words and the piece centred on the relationship between the two. *MSM* surprised audiences and critics with this shift in approach and even audiences familiar with DV8's previous work questioned the need to use trained dancers as performers and whether the work should be presented as a piece of dance. The piece also received huge critical praise and was described by critics as 'arresting', 'inventive', 'extraordinary' and 'alive' and Time Out London named it the 'Best performance of 1993'. However, much reception of the piece included comments on the lack of 'dance'.

> Its world première was presented as a big event of this year's Festival International de Nouvelle Danse in Montreal, prior to its British performances; but it defies you to call it dance. Instead, it is text-based theatre, with clambering about and movement images, but not a ghost of a step demanding dancers [...] But I found it gripping, illuminating and human. (Meisner 1993)

Clearly, Newson's intention to expand the relationship between language and movement by combining movement with verbatim material resulted in a major challenge to the understanding among audience and critic alike of what dance should look like, especially when compared to his previous work. The work was created and performed by a cast of mainly trained dancers, movement was present from the opening to the closing of the piece and several reviews of the piece refer to the performers as 'contortionists' or 'mountaineers'. However, this closer or more direct relationship to the spoken language seemingly complicated the ability for audiences to view the work as a piece of dance. This unsettled 'horizon of expectation', including the questioning of the right of the company to frame and present this performance as a piece of dance-theatre, perhaps indicates that DV8 had managed to achieve their aim to 'extend' the relationship between movement and recorded/spoken language and in doing so had further pushed the boundaries of dance-theatre to create a language of performance that managed to break through the already greatly flexible parameters of the genre of dance-theatre.

DV8's subsequent work, *Enter Achilles* (1995–1998), *Bound to Please* (1997), *The Happiest Day of My Life* (1999), *Can We Afford This/The Cost of Living* (2000), *The Cost of Living* (2003), *Just for Show* (2005) drew predominately on the choreographers' and performers' personal (and often exposing) reflections and revelations, overhead anecdotes and psychological research. These works reveal a switch back from the verbatim documentary/approach to the personal. Perhaps this switch was due to the fact that the work started looking at previously unexplored subject matter such as restrictive social etiquette, physical perfection and beauty, love and pretence, deception and honesty. Thus, by exploring new subject matter or considering personal relationships through a different focus, Newson returned to improvisation and a mixture of personal anecdote and fictional material.

In 2007, 14 years after the creation of *MSM*, with *To Be Straight With You* (2007), DV8 returned to the process of collecting recorded interviews to use as the starting point for choreography. In Newson's introductory speech for the National Theatre Live screening of *JOHN* (2014) (DV8 Physical Theatre, 2015), he stated that this move to working with verbatim material in 2007 was a result of his being tired of creating fictional work, claiming that he wanted to make work that was much closer to documentary. Returning to this process also meant revisiting the attempts to extend the way in which DV8's work can approach the relationship between language and movement through experimental practice. DV8's projects *To Be Straight With You* (2007), *Can We Talk About This?* (2011) and *JOHN* demonstrate the company's sustained commitment to investigating the collaboration between verbatim text and choreographed movement. Working with pre-existing verbatim material significantly changed the way the company approached the relationship between the language and the movement, and for the first time in his career, Newson altered the way he described his work by asserting that *To Be Straight With You* 'is a verbatim work with a strong physical theatre underpinning' (Newson 2007). By ascribing an underpinning role to movement Newson implies a shifting hierarchical relationship that places the verbatim text in a position of higher importance. Rather than aiming to tell a story through movement and draw on spoken language to support or fill in the gaps, where the movement struggles to tell the story, in *To Be Straight With You*, the movement is formed by the performers analysing the verbatim material and discovering ways of physically responding to, or translating, that material. Since 1993, when DV8 created *MSM*, there has been a significant change in the status of verbatim theatre. In 1993, verbatim theatre was being used by a few theatre companies in a narrow sense, such as Tricycle Theatre who mainly staged transcripts from legal trials, but when the company returns to use verbatim material in 2007, the use of verbatim material was widespread and diverse. A range of performance artists, play-based theatre, experimental theatre companies and community theatre companies drew on verbatim material and included the term 'Verbatim Theatre' in their promotional material.

In the creation processes for *To Be Straight With You, Can We Talk About This* and *JOHN* the recorded spoken language is the starting point for the choreographic process. The spoken material is collected, edited and structured before the creation of movement is approached. The movement material is created as a response to the recorded spoken language, the form of this response is a physical translation. Every single improvisational task takes place with the performers either listening to or listening to and speaking aloud the words of the recorded spoken language. Thus, both in the creation process and performance, the recorded or spoken language and the movement material are placed together and work as equal partners to create a specific form of performance material.

Translation as a Choreographic Approach

Discussing the research and development process for *To Be Straight With You*, Newson (2007) explains that, 'The themes behind this production are complex, sensitive and not easily translated into movement'. I would argue that since 2007, for DV8, translation has become a dramaturgical device/a choreographic practice. Every instance of creating a physical translation of the recorded spoken language was approached with the intention of placing the two together in performance. In DV8's work this double-voiced performance is either presented with the performer speaking the interview live while performing the movement translation or with the audio recording of the spoken language being played, while the performers perform the movement translation. An example of where the performer simultaneously speaks the interview and performs the translation is the scene in *To Be Straight With You* when Ankur Bahl performs exhausting movement with a skipping rope whilst also speaking the interview of an Asian man from Hull explaining his family's violent reaction to his telling them he was gay.

In *Can We Talk About This?*, an ensemble of performers shuffle in and around each other with a constant change of direction to the audio recording of Jeremy Paxman mediating between Anjem Choudhury and Maajid Nawaz on *Newsnight*. This is an example of movement translation being performed to the accompaniment of an audio recording. The fact that the verbatim text and choreographed movement are simultaneously presented in a double-voiced discourse is central to understanding the work and its potential for creating heteroglossic performance material. The recorded/spoken language and the movement material are viewed together, however, this does not mean that the relationship between the two is always harmonious. Is there a specific relationship between these two different forms of communication that, when combined, offer multiple perspectives which confront and undermine the concept of the existence of any single or concrete meaning?

The relationship between the recorded spoken words and the movement in *To Be Straight With You, Can We Talk About This?* and *JOHN* is constantly changing. The different movement responses present in their work provides an insight into the fact that, while DV8 use translation as a framework through which to view their choreographic practice, their approach to translating verbatim material is centred around the belief that the layering of a complex relationship between movement and language can allow a deeper connection and understanding of a subject, situation or person and their studio-based tasks are developed with the overarching intention to create movement that will illuminate the recorded spoken language. The choreographic translation could be divided into the following two areas:

1. Choreographic work that develops an awareness of the possibility of the different ways to respond to and negotiate with the verbatim

material (complementary, oppositional and the in-between space) included a focus on breaking-down the verbatim material into different parts (rhythm, meaning, tone, context).
2. Choreographic work that focus on physical restrictions as a way to offer an overarching physical metaphor to use in the translation process.

Different Ways to Stage Choreography and Verbatim Material Side-by-Side

In order to consider Newson's choreographic work, it is important to acknowledge that his choreographic interest lies in the role of movement in the production of meaning and communication in performance. Therefore, Newson works with his performers to make explicit the choreographic potential for adding to/complicating/undermining/highlighting the meanings present in the verbatim material. DV8's work is created within the belief that people instinctively interpret body language and DV8's choreographic approach is to see how far this body language can be pushed and extended in performance as a form of theatrical communication. In what could either be viewed as a direct attack on formalist choreographers who claimed dance to be an art form that should be detached from symbols and devoid of meaning, or an acknowledgement of the concept developed within the discourse of semiotics that nothing is omitted from semiosis, Newson (in Montgomery 2014) has stated that 'if people don't understand what's being said physically, I'm not interested'. As discussed in the introductory text, Newson's choreographic work is significantly influenced by the work of Bausch and the German *Tanztheater* tradition. Bausch, who trained under Kurt Jooss, a key practitioner of German expressionist dance, developed her own choreographic style that had deep roots in the expressionist dance movement of 1920s and 1930s Germany. As discussed in the introductory text, Elswit (2014) notes that it was the German expressionist choreographers creating work in the Weimar Republic who developed a detailed exploration of movement as a mode of communication and the ability of choreographic work to explore and address social, political and moral questions and subject matter. Newson's choreographic work is deeply rooted in and could be viewed as an extension of, the *Ausdruckstanz* and *Tanztheater* tradition that develops movement within a robust understanding that movement can be understood and 'read' by an audience.

Rather than allowing his performers to let their trained dancers' bodies simply respond to the material, Newson demands their constant critical awareness and analysis of that response. He expects his performers to consistently engage in an explicit dialogue with themselves, and with Newson as choreographer, about what the movement could communicate to an audience. If it is understood that movement can be viewed as an independent mode of communication, then the performance process of placing the verbatim material and its movement translation side-by-side in performance becomes a unique presentation of on stage translation in which their (English-speaking) viewers become a 'bilingual' audience able to read both languages. An awareness that the viewer will be able to access both modes of communication on stage places the translator in a unique position in which they can assume that the viewer will take part in creating meaning across and within the space in-between the different modes of communication and discover the gaps and slippage involved in the translation process. DV8 often presents movement that exists in a complex relationship with the recorded spoken language. This results in creating material that highlights translation as a form of dialogue and find ways to perform the gaps between the recorded/spoken language and the movement translation.

The choreography in *To Be Straight With You, Can We Talk About This?* and *JOHN* exists in a complex relationship with the recorded spoken language and this relationship shifts within each piece. Very simply, the choreography moves between existing in an obvious relationship, an opposite relationship or somewhere in the vast space in-between these obvious or opposite responses. Using the frame of heteroglossia (Bakhtin 1981) to understand this choreographic work, it can be understood that through offering multiple and different positions in the performance material rather than merging the two different forms of communication into one performance language Newson is choreographing material that aims to expose the polysemous makeup of meaning.

These three different responses to the verbatim material can be seen in DV8's performance work. An obvious response, or a moment when there is a clear connection between the spoken words and the movement can be seen in the scene in *To Be Straight With You* during which Bahl delivers the spoken words collected from an interviewee describing the fact that although he is married and has a family he visits gay clubs and is drawn to Bollywood music. As he delivers the speech, including the revelation that he cannot 'resist' music and dancing, he performs a vibrant and fluid duet with Langolf that is made up of Bharatanatyam movement. This movement complements and supports the words of the interview. An opposite response, during which the movement and words directly collide can be viewed in a scene in *Can We Talk About This?* when Joy Constantinides speaks the words of an interview collected with former British Labour Party MP Ann Cryer, while being moved around the space by Lee Davern. The speech Constantinides delivers describes how hard it was for Cryer to speak about and tackle the act of forced marriage in parliament. At the same time, she performs movement in which she maintains a relaxed and easy posture, holding a cup of tea, while being supported and moved fluidly around the space, both bodies working in perfect harmony, and Constantinides' weight being supported by Davern. The problematic and challenging relationships described in the interview are the clear opposite of the easy, supported and harmonious relationships involved in the movement material. As Constantinides delivers the lines 'I argued and argued for nine years', her body is supported in a sitting position as she is guided by Davern's weight to sit on his knee and she relaxes her weight into Davern, his foot supporting her under her armpit. The two bodies are having to share weight at times to move fluidly between movements, however, the movement is centred on Davern finding new ways of taking Constantinides' weight and allowing her to maintain a relaxed position. This fluid and soft duet between a male and female body that also provides a very different relationship than the relationships spoken about in the words of the speech in which we hear that 'It was very different talking to men, some men said forced marriage did not exist and was a figment of my imagination'.

A response that is situated in the space somewhere between an obvious and oppositional response can be found in a scene in *To Be Straight With You* during which Siobhan delivers speech taken from a man speaking at Hyde Park's Speakers Corner, while the rest of the cast perform constantly moving motifs that consist of pedestrian movement of sitting down, standing up, walking and moving the position of chairs. As Siobhan delivers text that includes an assertion that the Koran condemns homosexuality, there is no obvious or oppositional connection between this pedestrian group movement. The fact that the performers are constantly shifting position could be read as the shifting opinions of people and religions over time, but also could be understood as a comment on the speaker's inability to move from a particular position or could be viewed as the speakers search for a way to understand the changing culture. The repetition of people standing up and sitting down could be read as people's uncertainty about whether they want to or feel they are allowed to challenge this speech, or it could be understood as communicating that these listeners are changing their mind as to whether they agree or disagree with the speakers view depending on what they are hearing at that exact moment.

This approach to choreographing a physical translation of verbatim material, that rejects the verbatim practitioner's role as locating and reiterating a single meaning in the verbatim material, helps to challenge and open-out current practice in verbatim theatre. This attempt to practically and creatively explore the performer's different choreographic responses resonates with Tymoczko's (2007) aim to liberate translators from the 'false dictate to preserve meaning', thus empowering and producing creative practitioners. The choreographer/performer's role within this task is to explore different and divergent ways of responding to the source material. This approach, to find and then stage a range of responses to the verbatim material, echoes Bakhtin's (1981: 296) view that a text can contain 'the intention of the character who is speaking, and the refracted intention of the author'. This way of presenting movement and spoken language side-by-side thus contains the potential to create performance material that will allow different and separate positions to exist in the performance text and stage the negotiation between the different cultural, political, personal and philosophical positions present in the verbatim material and its movement translation. The dancer as translator is able to explore the different responses available to them and therefore can potentially address their own reaction and relationship to the words they are listening to. Thus, in an attempt to explore the different possible approaches to the verbatim material and stage them in a double-voiced discourse with each other, it becomes possible for this performance material to achieve what Batchelor (2008: 64) suggested was important, to 'highlight the hostile relationship between source and target text'.

This way of creating performance material allows the choreographer/performer to view the different responses available to them and therefore strengthens understanding of the translation process as a form of dialogue. This view of the choreographer/performer as embodying their response and using movement to speak back to the recorded language echoes Perteghella's (2013) assertion that the process of translation should be understood as a 'dialogic exploration of the text, which leads to its eventual transformation'. In her exploration of translation as a form of dialogue, she suggests that a translator's ability to respond 'even from a different, alternative and experimental perspective, provides a further development in the relationship between translator and text' and that these responses, even if they contain conflict, can allow the translator 'to enter into a dialogue [with the source text] in a more creative and critical way' (Perteghella 2013). If choreographers and performers working with verbatim text can draw on an obvious/opposite/in-between response while improvising/devising movement, then they have the potential to create performance material that is presented as a multi-voiced dialogue, in which the performers perform as readers, interpreters and commentators of the accompanying recorded/spoken language.

The creation and presentation of movement material that does not attempt a direct translation or exist in an easy relationship with the verbatim text resonates with Perteghella (2013), O'Sullivan (2012) and Tymoczko's (2007) call for creative translations that openly enter into a dialogue with the source text and has the potential to create 'dialogized' heteroglossic performance material that is aware of the 'competing definitions for the same thing'. The direct layering of the recorded/spoken language and the movement has the potential to foreground tensions between the verbatim material and its translation into performance material and reveal the creative play between these two different forms of communication (spoken language and movement). Participating in the task and spectating others perform the task brought to mind Carlson's (1992) assertion that a vital reason for employing a heteroglossic layering of languages in performance is to relinquish the monologistic authority over the text. In my own experience, it was the movement that contradicted or existed in this space in-between that stimulated an awareness of the different positions present in the material and offered a way of performing the dialectic between the verbatim material and its physical translation. Movement created in this way combined with the recorded/spoken language, contains the 'dialogized' heteroglossic possibilities. By focusing on the 'competing' the conflict, the fight between two different modes of communication to communicate the same thing can expose the ambiguous and complex nature of the meaning located in the performance material. It is when this movement material, containing choreography made by considering and including different perspectives to provoke a sense of the instability of meaning, is staged with its source material (the verbatim interviews) and presented as a double-voiced on stage translation that the layering of different modes of communications are allowed to simultaneously exist. It is this double-voiced discourse, placing the source text (verbatim interviews) and its translation (movement) side-by-side, demanding the viewer enter into a specific and active semiotic process, which suggests that the performance material created is inherently heteroglossic. Both the spoken word and the movement maintain their independence and rather than merging into one language, instead multiple perspectives are made present. The disruptive potential of the movement can be explored as the relationship between the verbatim material and movement translation is destabilised. This performance material can overtly reject an understanding of the translation process as the preservation of meaning, instead exposing translation in line with Batchelor (2008), Tymoczko (2007), Perteghella (2013) and O'Sullivan's (2012) understanding as a process of creative interpretation, interaction and dialogue between source text and translation. Reflecting on the possibilities of some of her own verbal and pictorial translations, Perteghella (2013) suggests that 'the juxtaposition of verbal and non-verbal texts in experimental translations allows us to explore different channels in which to express or contextualise our response of the text, even opening up a dialogue between modes'. In the work created in versions 2 and 3, it is perhaps the juxtaposition of the spoken language and the movement that allows this dialogic relationship to evolve. It is through witnessing this relationship that the viewer can move between what is being communicated by the words and the movement and perceive any tensions and gaps between the two.

This side-by-side movement translation of verbatim material can communicate that no single point of view is possible, sometimes even in one person's speech, let alone a translation. This double-voiced on stage translation performance material is created in the belief that the production is not the carrier, or conveyer, of meaning but rather, the provocation of meaning. The ultimate production of meaning is the responsibility of the individual viewer and this double-voiced performance material uses discontinuity, disruption and dislocation to encourage recognition of the heterogeneity of meaning. Therefore, the instability of the translation (the movement) becomes visible as viewers partake in the creation of meaning as unique individuals; different cultures and two different modes of communication confront each other. When there is not an obvious and complementary relationship between the words and the movement the viewer is being asked to co-construct meaning in the space where the two meet. When it is clear that the movement will not just reiterate or strengthen the meaning present in the spoken words, and that the spoken words might not reflect what the body is communicating, then the viewer must focus on what meaning/s are being created across and between the two different modes of communication. Placing the viewer in the position of noticing and reading the differences and negotiations at play in between the two forms of communication (Batchelor 2008: 64), thus 'essentially inviting readings of source texts and translations that are more open to ambivalence and subversion' (ibid.).

This way of choreographing verbatim dance-theatre brings up questions about when and why one might chose a complimentary, oppositional or in between response based on the translators individual opinions, perceptions and relationship to their source text. It also brings up some questions about how the different power relationships at play influence the movement translation of different interviews. For example, in DV8's work, the power relationships involved and the decision of whether to develop a complementary, oppositional or 'in -between' translation of an anonymous anti-gay rights protestor is very different to the translation of the words of a well-known politician or theorist. How will the performer's or choreographer's own culture, politics and philosophical position affect and shape an obvious, opposite or 'in between' response. In commenting on his own work, Newson does not address the difference between choreographing a response to opinions situated in line with or at odds with his own political or moral stance, however the fact that Newson creates movement material that exists in a complex relationship with the verbatim material, might be understood as a way to deal with the complex relationships involved between words and movement in translating vastly different social commentary, opinions and politics. Although this view establishes a tension with Newson's own commentary of his work, in which he claims his choreographic approach aims to be fair and respectful to all the individuals presented, I would assert that the choreographic material of *To Be Straight With You* and *Can We Talk About This?* illustrates that when Newson is choreographing a response to an interview with someone who shares similar values, beliefs or politics to himself he will often present movement material that perhaps exists in a complementary or obvious relationship with the verbatim material, which could perhaps be understood as producing monoglossic performance material, while when he is choreographing a response to an interview conducted with someone who has opposing values, beliefs or politics, he will combine this interview with movement that exists in a more complex relationship with the verbatim material.

For example, in a scene in *Can We Talk About This?* during which Siobhan performs a speech taken from a discussion between Mehdi Hassan, a political journalist, and Timothy Garton Ash, a professor of European Studies at Oxford University. During this discussion, part of the *Orwell Debate, 'What can't you speak about in the 21st century?'* (2010), Hasan points out that what we can talk about in the twenty-first century is always situated within certain parameters and that it is important to get the balance right about what can and cannot be said. This speech includes a warning against the concept of 'pure free speech' as something that is irresponsible and dangerous. As Siobhan speaks, Langolf and he perform an intricate and snake-like duet. The movement is mainly situated in the upper body and arms and is quick and awkward. The movement continuously moves in different directions, always coming to an abrupt finish and follows short and tight spatial patterns. The movement makes it look as if the two performers are moving in and out of small tight spaces and, upon reaching a dead end, calmly try to find a new space. The two move in and out of each other's space, constantly coming very close to making physical contact but always just avoiding doing so. As Siobhan delivers the lines 'we can all accept that there are restrictions on all speech. Pure free speech exists nowhere on earth nor should it', his feet and legs remain in a stiff and fixed position as his upper body lunges quickly to the side, moments after Langolf's upper body tips forwards and both performers' chests face the ceiling and roll through their bodies, moving them one step back, thus narrowly avoiding touching. The spoken language in this scene is taken from the speech of a well-known journalist and is taken from a public debate. Arguably, the relationship between Newson as an artist and Hasan as a writer is an equal one and Newson, although perhaps Newson regards Hasan as an expert in this field of research surrounding free speech. The movement translation of this speech appears to complement the idea being put forward by Hassan and could be understood as reinforcing the point being made that what people say must stay within certain boundaries. As we hear Siobhan speak Hasan's words and make the point that someone rejecting or threatening anybody's basic human rights should not have the right to air their views publicly, the performers' bodies stay within movement boundaries so that although performing different and strong movement, they never collide with each other. The force and speed of the movement makes it clear that if the bodies did collide it would be a violent collision, but they never do. When the spoken language is combined with this movement they appear to exist in a clear and complementary relationship to each other. Another example of this is when Ermira Goro performs the words from an interview with a man who explains that he faced the choice of either denying his sexuality or being kidnapped and assaulted, his body is violently and forcefully dragged around the space by three other performers. As Goro speaks the words 'They warned me, "you have to come and you have to obey"' his body is forcibly moved forward by the two male performers and thrown to the floor then moved into a new space. The movement performed both physicalises the threatened violence and reinforces the oppressed position of this man, as his body is guided around the space and he 'obeys'. Again, the spoken language and movement appear to exist in a complimentary relationship.

Although this performance material contains two different 'languages' or form of communication, the fact that they complement each other and there is no obvious conflict. The cooperation of the movement and speech here could be understood as what Bakhtin would have described as a merging to present a single or unified language. Whereas, as previously discussed in the case of the movement that accompanies the Christian protestor or the Muslim Preacher the movement does not exist in a complimentary relationship with the speech, rather offering a different position and different perspectives. Perhaps it is only the performance material that contains movement and spoken language that exists in a more complex relationship that contains the potential to remind the viewer to question both the mode of communication and their own role in the production of meaning. Perhaps as Bakhtin asserts that for dialogised heteroglossia to exist the writing must include different voices that are explicitly 'competing' to communicate 'different versions of the same thing', the performance material must contain moments where the movement and recorded/spoken language appear to exist in an antagonistic relationship for the viewer to be reminded of the polysemous nature of meaning.

Moving Physical Restrictions

To Be Straight With You, Can We Talk About This? And *JOHN* all contain numerous examples of the movement translations containing some form of physical restriction. For example, a performer keeping their back in contact with a wall, only moving their hands or performing an entire solo while skipping. There appears to be two ways in which these physical restrictions influence and shape DV8's performance material in their verbatim dance-theatre work. Firstly, the physical restrictions put in place challenge and extend the performers' use of their bodies and how the physical translations are approached. Secondly, the rules and parameters of the physical restriction at times act as an overarching physical metaphor for the movement translation of the interview material.

My own experience of experimenting with different physical restrictions in improvisations often means that performers are unable to develop or fall back on any movement habits or create any repeating movement phrases. When working as a choreographer, I often set performers improvisational tasks with a physical restriction and I am sure I am not alone in this practice. My experience has been that during a development or rehearsal process through using these physical restrictions, I observe my own and other performers' movement vocabulary go through a process of expansion as we develop an awareness of the infinite movement possibilities available in our own bodies when moving within certain restrictions. Interestingly, O'Sullivan, whose research in translation pedagogy includes developing innovative translation tasks that focus on releasing and encouraging creative translations, has developed a similar task to choreographers use of physical restrictions. In her article '*Playing With(out) the Dictionary: Using Constrained Literature in the Development of Transferable Skills for Translators*', O'Sullivan (2012) outlines her development of practical tasks for translation practitioners and students which, by focusing on different 'constraints', aim to encourage 'creative' and 'divergent' translation outcomes. O'Sullivan (2012: 1) proposes that 'translation and creative writing are two of the same activity' and asserts that translation exercises which include specific 'constraints' or rules provide a possible way to encourage creativity and enable 'a shift from source-language to target-language-based decision-making' (ibid). She argues that a focus on constraint can be a productive way of enabling creativity, noting that the two concepts have 'long been linked in both scholarship and translation practice' (O'Sullivan 2012: 2). O'Sullivan maintains that finding a way to encourage creative translations is essential for translation pedagogy.

> In my experience, students tend to be wary of any translational decision that exceeds the transfer of denotative and connotative meaning on the grounds that such acts of mediation are, in some ways, more than translation—which is of course not the case. (O'Sullivan 2012: 3–4)

She notes that this perspective is also held by the majority of professional translators.

> The Romantic author–creator-centred model of literary criticism has also resulted in translation analysis which takes the primacy and perfection of the source text for granted, and generates a persistent fantasy of the perfect, non-existent translation which renders everything in the source text without any additions. Meanwhile, creativity in translation comes under criticism when it develops into a tendency to 'improve on the author' (O'Sullivan 2006: 182), therefore situating itself outside translation proper. (O'Sullivan 2012: 5)

Her workshop-based exercises encourage translators to move away from looking to their fixed bilingual dictionary for translation solutions and to search instead for divergent and creative solutions. The workshop tasks put in place a range of constraints on the material features of the language used in the translation. For example, O'Sullivan (2012: 9–15) provides an extract of a piece of writing and asks the translators to translate the text adhering to certain rules such as: 'the text [translation] can only include one of the five vowel sounds'; or '[t]he translated paragraph must begin with the corresponding letter or character of the protagonist's name'; or '[t]he target text must omit four letters with equivalent fre-quency in the target language'; or '[t]he target text must omit the most common letter of the target language alphabet'. Below is an example of one of O'Sullivan's workshop tasks that includes this last aim, including details of the constraint and her reflection on the exercise.

Task 4: Lipogrammatic Translation

To translate a paragraph from George's Perec's lipogrammatic novel La disparition (Perec 1969: 17).

Anton Voyl n'arrivait pas à dormir. Il alluma. Son Jaz marquait minuit vingt. Il poussa un profound soupir, s'assit dans son lit, s'appuyant sur son polochon. Il prit un roman, il l'ouvrit, il lut; mais il n'y sai-sissait qu'un imbroglio confus, il butait à tout instant sur un mot dont il ignorait la signification. Il abandonna son roman sur son lit. Il alla à son lavabo; il mouilla un gant qu'il passa sur son front, sur son cou.

[LT: Anton Voyl couldn't get to sleep. He turned on [the light]. His Jaz [watch] read twenty minutes past midnight. He heaved a deep sigh, sat up in his bed, leaning on his bolster. He took a novel, he opened it, he read it; but he only picked up a confused imbroglio, he kept coming across a word whose meaning he didn't know.

He put down the book on his bed. He went to the basin, wet a flannel and wiped his forehead, his neck.]

Constraint: The target text must omit the most common letter of the target language alphabet.

Aim: To prompt students to draw on non-dictionary resources in the translation of a narrative text while conserving the register and coherence of the source text.

Methodology: Students are given a brief introduction to Perec and the novel, then a copy of the French text and a literal translation. This is usually done as a take-home exercise but can also be done in class if there is sufficient time.

Reflection: This exercise requires student translators to think outside the box and use a rather different series of linguistic tools. Translating lipograms in 'E' into English means that most past participles (ending in -ed) become unusable; this is also the case with the definite article 'the', and all third person singular and first person plural subject pronouns ('he, she, they, we'). The students' attempt to abide by the constraints of the exercise is likely to bring about shifts of denotative meaning, at least locally. Where the aim of the exercise is to produce a text whose losses are not at first evident—a mirror, as Briggs points out, of the problematic of translation itself (Briggs 2006: 44)—the translator's ingenuity is often stretched to its limit.

(O'Sullivan 2012: 13–14)

Similar to DV8's performance material that sees his performers translate the interview material by using only their hands or their head, or keep their back in contact with a wall, here O'Sullivan asks translators to write their translations by using a restricted alphabet, omitting certain letters. O'Sullivan's tasks and reflections provide an interesting framework through which to consider Newson's use of physical restrictions. In the same way that O'Sullivan aims to remove the translator's reliance on dictionaries, which she asserts will stretch 'the translator's ingenuity', Newson uses physical restrictions to restrict his performers' use of codified, pre-learnt or pre-rehearsed dance steps, demanding their translation is made up of new and inventive movement. The results can be seen across all of DV8's verbatim performance work. In *Can We Talk About This?* Langolf performs a translation of Roy Brown's speech outlining his proposal for discussing and confronting the UN's resolution 'Combating Defamation and Religion' which, he believes, 'prevents discussing human rights abuses in relationship to Sharia law', using only his hands. The movement is intricate, varied and complex and the choreography moves fluidly between different variations of outstretched fingers, pushing fists, complicated hand shapes, pointed and crushed fingers and attacking thumbs. It is clearly an example of 'hand choreography' pushed to its outer limits. Newson's rejection of codified dance techniques in favour of demanding his performers translate verbatim interview material within certain physical restrictions such as only moving the head, only using the arms, standing on their head, never touching the floor, means that the performers cannot consciously or unconsciously draw on previously learnt technique or movement to translate the verbatim material. O'Sullivan sees the 'constraints' of her developed tasks extending the translator's 'target language repertoire'. In the same way, a review of DV8's performance material and my own physical exploration of this device as a performer and choreographer suggests that these physical restraints in choreographic tasks result in the performer's movement vocabulary being continually challenged and extended. Just as Perteghella (2013) asserts that understanding creativity is an essential part of a translation helps translators to 'explore new spaces', O'Sullivan (2012: 6) proposes that these 'constraint' tasks will 'normalize creativity by considering it to be part of the act of writing/translation' thus legitimising and empowering translators to approach their work in a new and creative way.

As well as serving as a means of creating innovative movement content, these physical restrictions also work on another level. Often the physical restrictions in the movement translation of the verbatim material acts as an overarching physical metaphor.

For example, during a scene in *Can We Talk About This?* Langolf performs a speech taken from Martin Amis' speech delivered at the Institute of Contemporary Art in 2007, during which Amis asks the audience, 'Do you feel morally superior to the Taliban?' and includes his reflection that in the West we have 'succumbed to a pious paralysis', and are afraid to openly question the beliefs of Muslim extremists. The movement that Langolf performs moves fluidly up and down between positions in which he crosses his leg over his knee which then becomes the support base for his upper body to rest with one hand supporting his head in a well-known 'thinking image' to an upright position where he balances on his right leg as his left leg extends out to the side with a flexed foot and then, staying at hip level, slides behind and then in front of his right leg. This fluid upward and downward shifting is interrupted by sudden and curved movement in the torso. The entire movement sequence is performed by Langolf as he remains in contact with the wall behind him at all times, predominantly this takes the form of his entire back maintaining contact with the wall, while for brief moments this contact shifts to the backs of his arms or hands. The final sequence of this scene see's Langolf back loose contact with the wall as his body turns sideways, leaving his right shoulder, full arm and hand still in contact with the wall, next his shoulder and upper arm peel away as his lower arm and hand remain in contact, his lower arm then peels away and with only his hand remaining in contact he is able to take a small step away from the wall, and finally he removes his hand from the wall as he says 'We can't even say we are superior to the Taliban. Why can't we?'. This restriction put in place could be viewed as a metaphor for Amis having to 'watch his back', making sure that he can see his audience and defend himself for any possible attack. Or it could be read as a metaphor, for the fact that he is asking his audience to 'back up' his claims, he asks the audience to raise their hands if they do consider themselves to be morally superior to the Taliban and suggests that if that is the case they visually indicate that this is the case. DV8 have created some performance material that allows the movement and the recoded/spoken language to stand side by side and allow different meanings and positions to exist. In this double-voiced discourse both the verbatim spoken language and the movement translation are evident, and it is this staging, which presents the gaps and the slippage between the two, that has the potential to encourage the viewer to query and interrogate the meaning communicated in both the spoken words and the movement. DV8 have developed performance material that explore the subversive potential of the movement translation. The movement developed moves away from a direct complementary relationship with the verbatim material and presents imagery, metaphors and analysis that propose other and multiple meanings. This performance material highlights the complexity and instability of meaning, both in the source text (the verbatim interview material) and in the translation (the movement), by staging them side-by-side in a complex relationship to each other.

During DV8's *To Be Straight With You* these words were projected onto the back of the set, 'Over a period of 18 months DV8 conducted 85 interviews and a series of vox pops in London. Every word spoken on stage comes directly from the interviews. These are their words'. It could be argued that this ending statement that 'These are their words' is missing an important addition and it would be more appropriate for this statement to be changed to 'These are their words that have been chosen, edited and translated by us'. Bakhtin (1981) argued that by including multiple voices of varying perspectives and including those of 'ordinary' people an author could produce dialogised heteroglossic material. However verbatim theatre through its use of 'real' people's voices risks presenting those voices as 'their own' or unaltered, and therefore moves away from an understanding of a double-voiced discourse and towards a concept of a single-voiced discourse.

Heteroglossia, once incorporated into the novel (whatever the form of its incorporation), is *another's speech in another's language*, serving to express authorial intentions but in a refracted way it serves two speakers at the same time and expresses simultaneously two different intentions: the direct intention of the character who is speaking, and the refracted intention of the author (Bakhtin's 1981: 296). This understanding that performance material can simultaneously present two different intentions is at risk of being lost in verbatim theatre that does not attempt to explore and expose the performance artist's agency and acknowledge that in fact any performance material created is indeed the refracted intention of the choreographer/directors/writer.

Have DV8 been able to create verbatim dance-theatre works that highlight the complexity and instability of meaning, both in the source text (the verbatim interview material) and in the translation (the movement), by staging them side-by-side in a complex relationship to each other? Bakhtin suggested that exploring the use of a physical language, that had the potential to question and even parody other verbal languages, and including voices from different people in varying positions in society, which highlighted different dialects and perspectives, were rich devices for creating heteroglossic and dialogised heteroglossic material. An examination of DV8's use of movement as a mode of communication and the inclusion of verbatim material from a range of people from varying social and political positions supports Bakhtin's view as the use of these devices clearly creates heteroglossic material that highlights the polysemous and ambiguous nature of meaning. When movement language is presented as a translation of the spoken language and the two are performed side-by-side in a tense or antagonistic relationship, this can then strengthen the focus on the uncertain and opaque meaning/s being presented.

References

Bakhtin, M. (1981). Discourse in the Novel (translated from Russian by M. Holquist and C. Emerson). In M. Holquist (Ed.), *The Dialogic Imagination* (pp. 259–422). Austin: University of Texas Press.
Batchelor, K. (2008). Third Spaces, Mimicry and Attention to Ambivalence: Applying Bhabhian Discourse to Translation Theory. *The Translator, 14*(1), 51–70.
Bein' A Part, Lonely Art (DV8 Physical Theatre, 1985).
Bound to Please (DV8 Physical Theatre, 1997).
Can We Afford This/The Cost of Living (DV8 Physical Theatre, 2000).
Can We Talk About This? (DV8 Physical Theatre, 2011).
Carlson, M. (1992). Theater and Dialogism. In J. G. Reinelt & J. R. Roach (Eds.), *Critical Theory and Performance* (pp. 313–323). Ann Arbor: University of Michigan Press.
Deaths and Entrances (Martha Graham, 1943).
Dead Dreams of Monochrome Men (DV8 Physical Theatre, 1988).
Deep End (DV8 Physical Theatre, 1987).
DV8 Physical Theatre. (1993). *MSM Press Release* [online]. Available at: https://www.dv8.co.uk/projects/archive/msm/press-release. Accessed 10 Dec 2010.
DV8 Physical Theatre. (2015). DV8 Physical Theatre | Company Promo. YouTube [video]. 10 March. Available at: https://youtu.be/AsKtaMrxguE. Accessed 02 Jan 2018.

DV8 Physical Theatre. (2018). *Artistic Policy* [online]. Available at: https://www.dv8.co.uk/contact-dv8/artistic-policy. Accessed 8 Jan 2018.
Elemen T(h)ree Sex (DV8 Physical Theatre, 1987).
Elena's Aria (Anna Teresa de Keersmaeker, 1984).
Elswit, K. (2014). Watching Weimar Dance. Oxford: Oxford University Press.
Enter Achilles (DV8 Physical Theatre, 1995–1998).
If Only (DV8 Physical Theatre, 1990).
JOHN (DV8 Physical Theatre, 2014).
Just for Show (DV8 Physical Theatre, 2005).
Kontakthof (Pina Bausch, 2010).
Meisner, N. (1993). Review: From the Well of Loneliness. *The Times* [online]. Available at: https://www.dv8.co.uk/pages/review-the-times-from-the-well-of-loneliness. Accessed Nov 2010.
Montgomery, H. (2014). DV8: Three Decades of the Provocative Dance-Theatre Company. *The Independent* [online]. Available at: http://www.independent.co.uk/arts-entertainment/theatre-dance/features/lloyd-.
MSM (DV8 Physical Theatre, 1993).
My Body, Your Body (DV8 Physical Theatre, 1987).
My Sex Our Dance (DV8 Physical Theatre, 1986).
Newson, L. (1992). Strange Fish. *Dance & Dancers*, 10–13.
Newson, L. (1993). Lloyd Newson on Dance. *Dance Now*, 2(2), 11–13.
Newson, L. (1998). Lloyd Newson in Interview with Jo Butterworth. In J. Butterworth & G. Clarke (Eds.), *Dancemakers' Portfolio: Conversations with Choreographers* (pp. 115–125). Bretton Hall: Wakefield.
Newson, L. (2007). *Q&A with Lloyd Newson—To Be Straight with You* [online]. Available at: http://www.dv8.co.uk/about_dv8/interview_to_be_straight_with_you_q_a. Accessed 20 Dec 2010.
Newson, L. (2008). *DV8's To Be Straight With You: Dancing Against Prejudice*, [online]. Available at: http://www.guardian.co.uk/stage/2008/oct/27/dv8-straight-with-you. Accessed 20 Dec 2010.
O'Sullivan, C. (2012). Playing with(out) the Dictionary: Using Constrained Literature in the Development of Transferable Skills for Translators. *The Interpreter and Translator Trainer*, 6(2), 237–263.
Perteghella, M. (2013). Notes on the Art of Text Making [Blog]. *The Creative Literary Studio*. Available at: https://thecreativeliterarystudio.wordpress.com/tag/manuela-perteghella/. Accessed 6 Jan 2014.
The Cost of Living (DV8 Physical Theatre, 2003).
The Happiest Day of My Life (DV8 Physical Theatre, 1999).
To Be Straight With You (DV8 Physical Theatre, 2007).
Totenmal (Mary Wigman, 1930).
Tymoczko, M. (2007). *Enlarging Translation, Empowering Translators*. Manchester: St Jerome Publishing.

CHAPTER 4

Making Verbatim Dance-Theatre

Abstract McCormack offers a summary and reflection of her own choreographic practice in the field of verbatim dance-theatre. The chapter outlines the Practice as Research project *Cathy Come Home* (2011–2012) during which McCormack choreographed a verbatim dance-theatre work in response to Jeremy Sandford and Ken Loach's *Cathy Come Home* (BBC 1966) and a series of collected interviews with over 50 people, including those facing current housing issues themselves, housing support workers and academic researchers in housing law. The chapter examines the role of choreographer as translator and includes detailed examples of choreographic exercises developed by McCormack in an attempt to explore ways of translating spoken words to choreographed movement. 'Making Verbatim Dance-Theatre' concludes with an analysis of the relationship between verbal language and choreographed movement that exists in a double-voiced discourse in live performance and its potential to reveal and stage the choreographer's own agency.

Keywords Choreography · Improvisation · Verbatim theatre Translation

Cathy Come Home

Cathy Come Home (2012) is a Practice as Research project exploring approaches to contemporary verbatim dance-theatre, resulting in a piece of live performance. *Cathy Come Home* enquires into different possible choreographic translation approaches to verbatim interview material and the combination of recorded/spoken language and movement in and through practice. As a response to Jeremy Sandford and Ken Loach's *Cathy Come Home* (BBC 1966), I met and collected interviews with over 50 people, including those facing current housing issues themselves, housing support workers and academic researchers in housing law. The live performance was presented to a public audience in contemporary arts and performance venue, Arnolfini, Bristol in May 2012. As part of the project, in addition to creating *Cathy Come Home*, which was performed by professional performers, I invited three local young companies, 1625 Independent People (directed by Added Insight), Kinesis Youth Dance Company (directed by Julia Thorneycroft) and Travelling Light Theatre Company (directed by Craig Edwards), to produce their own response to the 1966 film.

These pieces of film, dance and performance were presented as the first half of the evening alongside *Cathy Come Home* at the Arnolfini. These pieces of performance framed the viewing of *Cathy Come Home* in a particular way. I hoped that by sharing the work of these young people, some of whose interviews are included in *Cathy Come Home*, the audience would start to think about the multiple different positions existing in the performance. Also, by introducing these contrasting pieces of work as different responses in different performance languages to the same material, I hoped to introduce the idea that the translations of interviews in *Cathy Come Home* should be viewed as only one potential translation in one possible language and from one particular perspective.

Perteghella (2013) suggests that there are two main reasons why translations should be understood as personal texts. Firstly, the decision to translate a certain text is important and secondly, the translator's unique relationship with their source text will result in a particular, and thus a personal, translation. She borrows Bassnett's (2006) concept of 'falling in love' to explain that a translator will 'inhabit' and 'live intimately' with the source text in order to create their translation.

In line with Perteghella's suggestions here, I will briefly explore my decision to use *Cathy Come Home* (1966) as a starting point to collect and translate interviews on the theme of homelessness. According to data published by the Department for Communities and Local Government in 2011, 69,460 children were living in homeless households in England and 48,510 households were listed as homeless by local authorities. Living in private rented housing myself, I was increasingly aware of the growing cost of renting and the impact that demand for housing was having on the condition of rented housing available. Planning to start a family and looking for a two bedroom property close to the centre of Bristol within our budget based on the combined above average earnings of a full-time teacher and part-time FE lecturer, it was difficult to find accommodation in a safe and healthy condition. I understood we were not in a unique position, and Campbell Robb (in Rogers 2012), Chief Executive of Shelter confirms in 2012 many 'ordinary' families were struggling to secure appropriate housing.

Increasing numbers of ordinary families are falling victim to our housing crisis. Some may be priced out of the housing market, forced to bring up their families in a revolving door of private let after private let.

While my understanding grew that 'ordinary' and middle-class people were struggling to find secure housing, so was the press coverage of the British coalition government's proposed cuts to housing benefit that would come into effect on 1 January 2013. Housing campaigners, including those from Shelter and Crisis, were suggesting a 'devastating' impact on homelessness statistics. The Chief Executive of Crisis, Lesley Morphy (in Rogers 2012), predicted a severe change to homelessness in Britain.

Our worst fears are coming to pass. We face a perfect storm of economic downturn, rising joblessness and soaring demand for limited affordable housing combined with government policy to cut housing benefit plus local cuts to homelessness services.

This severe warning from frontline housing campaigners, coupled with my own wish to secure a home for my family, connected strongly with my memory of having watched the film *Cathy Come Home* (1966) earlier in the year and I felt that this was a story that needed to be kept alive and continue to be told. *Cathy Come Home* (1966) blurred the lines between fiction and documentary, combining written dialogue with improvised dialogue and dialogue and sound collected from 'ordinary' people on location. As I began volunteering with 1625 Independent People, an organisation that supports young people aged 16–25 who are experiencing housing issues, I met and talked to a variety of people with a wide range of experiences that would add to, up-date and extend the narratives presented in Sanford and Loach's story of Cathy and Reg. I collected interviews with housing officers, housing support workers, people experiencing housing issues themselves, academic researchers in housing law and relationship therapists dealing with relationship breakdown caused by stress due to housing issues. In line with Perteghella's assertion that a translator will 'fall in love', 'inhabit' and 'live intimately' in the translation process, I 'fell in love' with *Cathy Come Home* (1966) as a piece of storytelling that managed to focus on individual experience to communicate a wider socio-political concern. I 'fell in love' with the idea of hearing and making people listen to the narratives of individuals living amongst us in our city (Bristol) who were struggling to find a secure home. The next process was to 'inhabit' these oral recordings by embodying and moving the recordings in the way my body, as a dancer, knows how to make sense of the world around me.

Almost every interview conducted for *Cathy Come Home* resulted in over an hour of recorded material. The process of collecting an hour long interview, editing this into a shorter extract and then translating this into movement, embodied Tymoczko's (2007: 71) reference to the process captured in the Igbo words *tapia* and *kowa*, meaning 'break it up and tell it (in a different form)'. As well as developing ways of translating the recorded spoken language 'in a different [movement] form' during the initial six weeks of solo choreographic experimentation, I also explored physical ways of 'breaking apart' this source material. My body and the recorded spoken language in its entire unedited form inhabited the studio as I improvised within the physical constraints I had set, namely that my body should move only when I was most intrigued, interested, angered or otherwise affected by the interview I was listening to and should stay still when I felt less of a connection or impulse to move. Although this process supported my active listening to the interview material and deepened my understanding of the material, as the person who chose the subject matter and collected the individual interviews, I moved to almost the entire fifty hours of recorded interview material during these improvisations. Having established the choreographic technique of watching or taking part in a lengthy improvisation, then drawing on my visual or kinaesthetic memory directly after the improvisation to recall the moments which I wanted to keep, and then using these to create a short phrase of movement, I adapted this process as an editing technique for the interviews. I would listen to the interview while moving and then directly after, would write down what I remembered from the interview and use this as the outline for editing the audio recording. During this process, it became clear through my 'breaking apart', selection and editing of the material that I was developing a performance script which centred on sudden and unexpected loss, loss of home, loss of partner, loss of identity, as well as reflections on the physical feelings of having to fight for something. The narratives selected for inclusion in the performance script also emphasised that homelessness can happen suddenly, with only a short sequence of bad luck and lack of immediate support resulting in a significant change in someone's housing status. In line with Sanford and Loach's aim of making a wider BBC watching audience aware that a British working family could easily subside into homelessness without sufficient state support, my aim was to bring the experiences of these local young people experiencing homelessness to a contemporary arts venue (the Arnolfini) which historically has a predominantly middle-class audience, thus reiterating this point by performing those moments in which people move from what such an audience would view as a secure housing status to homelessness. This process of course highlights the development of my own agency in the shaping of the performance script.

Cathy Come Home

> A unitary language is not something given [dan] but is always in essence posited [zadan]—and at every moment of its linguistic life it is opposed to the realities of heteroglossia. But at the same time, it makes its real presence felt as a force of overcoming this heteroglossia, imposing specific limits to it, guaranteeing a certain maximum of mutual understanding and crystallising into a real, although still relative, unity. (Bakhtin 1981: 270)

Cathy Come Home was approached from the position of practitioner and theorist and can essentially be understood as an exploration of choreographic processes that contain the potential to undermine and rupture any sense of a unitary language. This chapter will include a critical reflection of the practice undertaken and developed, focusing on the choreographic processes produced for translating verbatim recorded/spoken language into performance material. The chapter will interrogate the role of choreographer as translator, and focus on finding different ways of staging an awareness that 'competing definitions for the same thing' exist in the performance material. The development of ways to approach choreographic translation which avoid the creation of monoglossic performance material will be underpinned by the call from Batchelor (2008), Loffredo and Perteghella (2006), Tymoczko (2007) and O'Sullivan (2012) for creative translation practice that acknowledges and unveils the translator's subjective position and which views translation as a form of dialogue. Also relevant is the challenge from Renov (1993), Rabiger (2004) and Grierson (1966) to create a documentary practice that attempts to reveal and include complex personal perceptions. The final reflections will be on what processes were developed to produce 'dialogized' heteroglossic performance material and whether a focus on specific structural choreographic devices which play with and expose the double-voiced discourse can answer Batchelor's (2008: 63) call for 'a translation solution that can preserve not just the slippage, but also the disruptive power of the slippage' and Bottoms' call for Verbatim theatre practitioners 'to acknowledge their own highly selective manipulation of opinion and rhetoric' (Bottoms 2006: 57).

The central aim of this practice as research was to find ways to approach movement translations of the recorded/spoken language that would secure the translation in a dialogic context and produce performance material that could be understood as containing what Bakhtin termed dialogised heteroglossia. Achieving this aim was undertaken in three stages. Firstly, collect and include verbatim material from a range of different individuals from varying social, economic and political positions; secondly, develop movement translation tasks that will enable the translator to enter into a dialogue with the recorded/spoken language, with a focus on creating material that exists in an oppositional or ambiguous relationship with its source text; thirdly, experiment with and develop ways of exposing, the choreographer's agency in the performance material. *Cathy Come Home* was an attempt to produce performance material that could be understood as dialogized heteroglossia. In the same way as the fabliaux and schwänke identified by Bakhtin collected and included a variety of voices from a cross section of society, so the verbatim language was collected and included from artists (choreographer, performers, film director, film actors), scholars, young people of different races and nationalities who were experiencing housing issues, journalists (right and left wing) and a range of professionals (housing officers, support-workers and counsellors). The creative process experimented with a number of different ways to choreograph a movement translation of the recorded spoken language which would release the movement's subversive potential, by interrupting any view that a single-voice could exist. The subsequent account does not include an analysis of the entire performance text created; however, it considers each different choreographic device developed and explored. Many different scenes were created using the same choreographic tasks and therefore this chapter discusses one representative example scene developed through each different approach.

Task 1: Field, Tenor, Mode

Inspired by O'Sullivan's (2012) development of translation tasks that impose specific constraints on which material features of the language can be used in the translation process, Newson's similar use of physical restrictions on which part of the body can be used to generate a translation of material and Tymoczko's (2007: 71) reference to the Igbo words *tapia* and *kowa*, meaning 'break it up and tell it (in a different form)', a framework for 'breaking down' the recorded spoken language was established to create a movement translation which would disrupt any complementary relationship between the recorded/spoken language and the movement, thus disrupting the monoglossia. I developed a growing interest in different methods of breaking down the recorded spoken interviews and I became specifically interested in what exploring a physical linguistic analysis of the material. The focus for the movement translation changed from interview to interview. Whereas for some of the verbatim material, the company chose to translate the tone of interviewee's voice, for other material the focus became the vocabulary used or the rhythm of the speech. The choice of focus appeared to be intuitive on the part of the choreographer rather than through any process of exploring options and arriving at a conscious decision.

In preparation for *Cathy Come Home* workshops, I became interested in developing a devising process that could enable the exploration of different aspects of all the verbatim material. In the studio, I began exploring physical tasks that focused on one aspect of the recorded spoken language at a time and in an attempt to find a clear focus for these improvisations I looked to models of linguistic analysis. The fleeting experience of participating in this task, using music instead of recorded language as the source material inspired me to consider the possibility of breaking down the recoded spoken language into all its separate parts.

Reflecting on a task in which I improvise a response to a different aspects of a piece of music, I realised that when considering my physical response I thought about the rhythm of the music, my emotional response to the musical tone, my understanding of the context or history of the music, my own personal historic or contextual connection to the music and the meaning located in the lyrics. My response varied depending on which aspect of the music I focused on. Using Elsie Carlisle's 1926 recording of *I Love My Baby (and my baby loves me)* as an example, my obvious physical response could include tapping my foot or shrugging my shoulders in direct timing with the rhythm of the piano; the light jumping of my feet to the excited and upbeat tone of the vocal melody; bouncing outward heel kicks informed by my knowledge of 1920s dance styles; the sliding and rolling on the floor informed by my memory of watching a young boy dance to this song at a friend's wedding; or a forceful backwards motion emerging from my cheek and hand, informed by my interpretation of the lyric 'He gives me kisses, each one is a smack'. Reflecting on this exercise, I started to conceive a physical analysis of recorded spoken language that could potentially be based on the framework of linguistic analysis. This idea of a physical linguistic analysis informed some of the workshops developed for the creation of *Cathy Come Home*.

This concept of taking apart, or unfolding, the source text also resonates with Perteghella's assertion that in order for a translation to enter into a rich discussion the process must start with an 'understanding' of the source text, a process of 'unwrapping the textual meanings', which also includes 'identifying the stylistic devices used' (Perteghella 2013). This process of taking apart and understanding the text is a process of 'opening up' the text but even at this stage Perteghella (2013) suggests it is also a process of 'incorporating our response and initiating a conversation with the text'. A translation that is first based on a deep exploration of the source text, even if it then diverges into new material, also aligns with Bakhtin's understanding of 'fertilized ground' in which heteroglossia can grow. In an attempt to break apart the recorded spoken language to focus on a single aspect, I wanted to explore whether I could devise physical tasks inspired by Systemic-Functional Linguistics, first developed by Halliday, McIntosh and Stevens (1964). Halliday (1978) held that a text could be analysed by examining its field, tenor and mode. Following Halliday's framework, I began to develop a triadic framework for creating movement from recorded spoken language. The intention here was not to create a rigorous and full linguistic analysis, but to borrow this mode of breaking the language down in order to find multiple ways for the movement to disrupt and collide with the recorded/spoken language. Thus, certain aspects of this framework have been included or left out, according to what was felt to enhance the potential to produce a creative choreographic response.

The field of discourse refers to the content of the text and the vocabulary used. For example, repetition of words or ideas, rhythm, informal/formal register, type of language (poetic, simple), contradictions in meaning, personal/public use of vocabulary or tone. The tenor of discourse looks at who is engaged in the text and the relationships involved. For example, status between people (verbal discourse, interview, interrogation), the nature of relationships (tense, easy, playful). The mode of discourse examines the channel of the text and its effect by determining whether it is 'didactic, therapeutic, persuasive, expository, and the such like' (Halliday and Hasan 1989: 12). For example, if it is a stream of consciousness, lesson, explanation, confession, etc. The development of this framework also draws on Laban's (1971) ideas of how to articulate movement analysis, in particular his use of identifying movement initiation, effort, shape change, special intentions and relationships, in movement material. I hoped that the application and adaptation of Halliday's framework might provide a way to approach translating verbatim material and offer sways to create movement that exists in a significant relationship and therefore has the potential to enter into valid conflict with the recorded spoken language, thus strengthening and deepening the heteroglossic potential of the performance material.

A task was developed that initially asked the mover to listen to a section of verbal language through headphones and focus on identifying the mode of the text. The mover was asked to experiment with and explore a number of physical restrictions that might make sense as a metaphor for this identified mode of the text. Some examples of physical restrictions explored throughout this process are, hand and arm movement being performed behind the back when working with a speech that the mover suggested was a 'reluctant confession'; the body and limbs only being able to move in straight lines to explore a speech identified by the mover as a 'direct attack'; movement only created in the fingers to explore a speech which the mover identified as a 'didactic lesson'; and having to constantly be jumping to explore a speech that the mover identified as being a 'debate' (Table 4.1).

Table 4.1 Mode

1(a)	Mode Channel of the text 'didactic, therapeutic, persuasive, expository'? Debate? Stream of consciousness? Lesson? Explanation? Confession? Sermon? Political address? Spontaneous or Rehearsed?	Locate a physical restriction Restriction of part of body used? Restriction of space used? Restriction of contact to physical object or performer?

Having located a physical restriction, the mover was asked to maintain this while taking part in seven further improvisations, each with a different focus. Borrowing the structure from Newson's choreographic task, the movers were asked to develop a complementary, oppositional and in-between response for each different focus. However, the use of the in-between here did not refer to a response existing outside of the complementary or oppositional but meant a response attempting to physically interpret the dialogue between the complementary and oppositional response. The aim here was to create a movement translation which, by recognising different perspectives and focusing on the dialogue between these different positions, would achieve an 'awareness' of competing responses in the way Bakhtin highlighted as essential to create dialogised heteroglossia. This dialogised heteroglossia attacks the idea of any one voice or perspective being the single or correct view. This focus became increasingly important as the creation process progressed, as it was clear that there was not one single reason for the rise in homelessness, there was not one single definition of the condition and that in order to enter into a significant dialogue about the issue of homelessness the complexity of the situation needed to be acknowledged (Table 4.2).

In the workshop process, I performed this task as the mover responded to a recorded discussion on BBC Radio 4 between Women's Hour presenter, Jenni Murray and Janice Atkinson, a British journalist who writes for the Daily Mail Online. This discussion followed an interview with a woman named Lesley, a mother of four children, who describes in emotional terms being unable to feed herself and her husband without the use of food bank vouchers from the charity Barnardos, because she spends their weekly budget on healthy food for her children.

Table 4.2 Field, tenor, mode

Task	Field/tenor/mode The aspect of the verbal language that will be the focus of the improvisation	Aspect of the movement that will be the focus of the translation
2(a)	Field	Restriction: Must focus on the rhythm and the temporal aspect of the movement
	Rhythm	Sustained–Sudden Slow–Fast Steady–Building
2(b)	Field	Restriction: Must focus on the effort of the movement
	Tone	Weight: Heavy–Light Flow: Bound–Free
2(c)	Field	Restriction: Must focus on the type of movement
	Type of vocabulary used	The initiation of movement: which part of the body does the movement come from?
2(d)	Field	Restriction: Must focus on the movement sequence and patterns
	Repetition of words or ideas	Is the movement made up of a small number of repeated and developed movements? Is the movement sequence made up of all different movements?
2(e)	Field	Restriction: Must focus on the spatial directions of the movement and the pathways
	Personal/public use of vocabulary	Direct–Indirect
3(a)	Tenor	Restriction: Must focus on the relationships between the different bodies in the space and the shape quality of the movement
	Power relationships	Height: The use of levels of each body in space Proximity: Where are the different bodies in the space?
	The status between people (verbal discourse, interview, interrogation)	Sinking–Rising? Spreading–Enclosing? Retreating–Advancing?
3(b)	Tenor	Restriction: Must focus on the contact between the different bodies in the space
	The nature of relationships (tense, easy, playful)	Do the bodies share weight? Is there any manipulation of one body: Tense, playful, strong, light?

Lesley has a middle-class accent and describes being a working mum and self-employed business owner, before having twin babies. The speech preceding this is also included in the performance text immediately before this scene. A transcription of this speech, as it is heard on the soundtrack in performance, can be found below.

> *Jenni Murray:* Janice, why have you been sceptical about the idea of parents missing meals to feed their children?
>
> *Janice:* There are some people who are going to be losing their jobs in the current climate, I absolutely accept that. But it is about managing budgets and what we have to look at Jenni is why we have these costs okay? So your interviewee there, she was clearly making the most of her budget but um I would argue that most people are not making the most of their budgets. You can go into Sainsbury's or Tesco's and you can buy a chicken for £3. And you can eke out three meals out of that, you can have roast chicken, you can have soup and you can have sandwiches. A lot of your people online I noticed they were talking about buying bags of apples. Now If I go to the supermarket I don't buy a bag of apples. Now this morning online on Tesco's a bag of eight apples was £3.29, now if you buy a bag of 8, or you buy 8 loose apples that's £2.28, now there's a big difference in that.

Table 4.3 shows an example of the application of this task to the choreographic process.

The performers were invited to observe the three different improvisations and reflect on which restriction they understood as connecting with the material. Five of the performers selected the third restriction, suggesting that it gave the sense of a driving body unable or unwillingly to stop and look at any other point of view. One performer selected the first restriction, suggesting that it connected with their sense that this speaker was uninhibited in assuming a lack of intelligence in their audience. The next part of the task was undertaken within the third restriction of having to perform a travelling movement following a narrow straight pathway (Table 4.4).

In performance, this section will be known as 'Apples'. The movement chosen to be combined with this speech, which was played in the soundtrack, experimented with the potential of movement to play a subversive role. The physical analysis of the speech had deepened an understanding of the speech and reveals that Janice takes a defensive position which is limiting, but helps her avoid conflicting thoughts and uneasy emotions. She has devised a rigid and narrow internal dialogue

4 MAKING VERBATIM DANCE-THEATRE   101

Table 4.3 Mode in practice

1(a)	Mode Channel of the text 'didactic, therapeutic, persuasive, expository'? Debate, stream of consciousness, lesson, explanation, confession, sermon, political address?	Dogmatic. The speech shows no interaction at all and the continuous flow of words indicates no desire to interact with the other speakers we know are present in the recording studio. Although this is supposed to be a panel discussion concerning food poverty, this speech is delivered as if it is a lecture and designed to teach two different groups of people the lesson that individual correct financial planning is the solution to poverty, (1) Those who spend their money poorly, thus unhelpfully placing themselves in the position of needing to use food banks and (2) Those who believe these people need state or charity support, rather than an education in financial planning Three different physical restrictions were experimented with before one was selected to be used for the rest of the task 1. Only including movement that originates from the index finger to act as a metaphor for the 'finger wagging' lecture 2. Having to keep my nose in contact with the wall at all times, to act as a metaphor for a lecture that doesn't include or reference anyone else's ideas 3. Having to continuously keep moving along a straight and narrow pathway to act as a metaphor for this rigid and focused lecture

that lacks critical thinking. She makes links to her own experience and demonstrates no empathy or social perspective. She presents a rigid and simplistic argument that draws from her own personal limited experience of how she herself saves money when shopping. The repeated use of the pronoun I, for example when Janice states that 'Now If I go to the supermarket I don't buy a bag of apples', reveals her desire to understand this situation through her own experience. Her speech and her use of simple vocabulary and a simplistic argument divides the world into good and bad and cannot imagine a third position which is to accept that there is no easy right or wrong but a far more complex, compassionate

Table 4.4 Field, tenor, mode in practice

Task	Field/tenor/mode	Physical Restriction: Movement must constantly travel forwards and be situated with a narrow straight pathway
2(a)	Field Rhythm	Restriction: Must focus on the rhythm and the temporal aspect of the movement Sustained–Sudden Slow–Fast Steady–Building The rhythm of the spoken language began as even and quick and towards the end of the speech the pace of the spoken words built to a climax Complementary: I moved my body along the restricted pathway only moving in direct correlation with the rhythm of the speaker's voice and holding stillness in moments of silence Oppositional: I played with developing a contradictory rhythm that was slow and used long moments of stillness, which directly contradicted the building and driving rhythm of the speech In-Between: I experimented with moving between a frantic and accelerated speed with sudden and uneven moments of absolute stillness
2(b)	Field Tone	Restriction: Must focus on the effort of the movement Weight: Heavy–Light Flow: Bound–Free The tone of the speaker's voice was sharp, light-hearted and superior Complementary: The movement used moments of relevé and small jumps and minimal weight was given to the movement, thus creating light movement that complemented the light-hearted tone. In the two moments when the speaker is on the verge of laughing before continuing with her speech I created a high jump during which my toes drew a circle in the air Oppositional: I applied a low plié to the movement, as I moved my feet stamped down into the floor and the flow of the movement was heavy and bound. My limbs stayed close and heavy as if supported by my torso In-Between: this improvisation explored movement that held a high level of tension and appeared to move awkwardly through a treacle-like substance. The flow remained bound, but occasionally the legs would attempt to move as far away from the other, moving forcefully and heavily through the space

(continued)

Table 4.4 (continued)

Task	Field/tenor/mode	Physical Restriction: Movement must constantly travel forwards and be situated with a narrow straight pathway
2(c)	Field	Focus on the type of movement The initiation of movement: which part of the body does the movement come from?
	Type of vocabulary used	The type of vocabulary used in this speech was simple, no technical or complex vocabulary was used. The hegemonic language of capitalism was used including the names of two of Britain's leading corporations Tesco's and Sainsbury's Complementary: This response was a playful one, that tried to mime or make an obvious connection to each of the words spoken, complementing the simple vocabulary used. The intention for each movement originated in the head as if a small head nod gave way to each movement Oppositional: This improvisation experimented by creating positions in which every part of the body was doing a different thing. A different movement initiated from every part of the body. These positions were made more and more complex until I lost my balance. These series of movements often began with the limbs and moved on through the body, ending with each finger attempting to curl or point or twist in a different position In-Between: This improvisation explored my focus looking around the room then using the image of an impulse coming from someone else position in the room and exploring that position in my own body
2(d)	Field	Restriction: Must focus on the movement sequence and patterns
	Repetition of words or ideas	Is the movement made up of a small number of repeated and developed movements? Is the movement sequence made up of all different movements? This speech is made up of the repetition of the same idea that parents who are 'claiming' to not be able to afford enough food to feel their family are victims of poor spending and financial planning. The idea 'I would argue that most people are not making the most of their budgets' is explored in different varieties, but is never extended Complementary: This improvisation developed a short sequence of six different movement selected from the previous improvisations and repeated the phrase six times Oppositional: This improvisation started with one movement and explored developing and adding to that movement accumulatively, with a clear progression of movement In-Between: During this improvisation I created a sequence of movement that started with one movement then developed the movement in three stages then moved onto the next

(continued)

Table 4.4 (continued)

Task	Field/tenor/mode	Physical Restriction: Movement must constantly travel forwards and be situated with a narrow straight pathway
2(e)	Field	Restriction: Must focus on the spatial directions of the movement and the pathways
	Personal/public use of vocabulary	Direct–Indirect
		This speech was addressed to the radio host as well as a public audience
		Complementary: This improvisation played with the movement originating close to my body and then moving out into the space, creating wide open positions
		Oppositional: This improvisation experimented with movement that was directed into my body, moving from the outside in
		In-Between: The movement developed here originated close to my body open out in direct pathways and then as if bouncing back came back to me this time in a slightly curved pathway
3(a)	Tenor	Restriction: Must focus on the relationships between the different bodies in the space and the shape quality of the movement
	Power relationships	Height: The use of levels of each body in space
		Proximity: Where are the different bodies in the space?
	The status between people (verbal discourse, interview, interrogation)	Sinking–Rising?
		Spreading–Enclosing?
		Retreating–Advancing?
		The speech takes a superior air and there is a clear dismissal of any views other than her own. She uses the radio host's name in a patronising way, for example when she says, 'what we have to look at Jenni [pause] is why we have these costs [pause] okay?'. The repetition of the rhetorical question 'okay?' following the introduction of very simple ideas is clearly patronizing. Also the use of the term 'I've noticed some of *your people* [my emphasis] on the internet' works to place these people she refers to in a low status position
		In order to explore the relationships here, I placed Tilly Webber in the space and asked her to perform some of the movement created as the translation of Lesley's speech from the previous section
		Complementary: The movement sequence was performed while moving towards Webber, increasing the height of the movement and closing in on her space
		Oppositional: The movement sequence was performed starting at a high level and sinking down to floor movement while at the same time moving away from Webber
		In-Between: This improvisation experimented with travelling towards Webber while the level of the movement continued to sink

(continued)

Table 4.4 (continued)

Task	Field/tenor/mode	Physical Restriction: Movement must constantly travel forwards and be situated with a narrow straight pathway
3(b)	Tenor The nature of relationships (tense, easy, playful)	Restriction: Must focus on the contact between the different bodies in the space Do the bodies share weight? Is there any manipulation of one body: Tense, playful, strong, light? The nature of the relationships are tense here as the listener is aware of the patronizing tone of the speaker. The speaker is completely disinterested in engaging anyone else in conversation or reflecting on any other viewpoints Complementary: This improvisation explored no contact made between the bodies on stage and no focus on the other body in the space, even when moving close to this other body Oppositional: This improvisation experimented with me carrying Webber on my back while trying to perform the movement sequence In-Between: This improvisation explored performing the movement in unison with five other performers while making no contact with Webber but maintain a focus on her at all times

space which accepts ambivalence. Janice's speech suggests that she quickly wants to label people as fitting into clear categories of 'managing their budgets' or 'not managing their budgets' and her defended and rigid tone makes it clear that she does not want to enter into any discussion that would complicate her view.

I experimented with combining this speech with movement that would expose and parody this position and through the use of complex and tangled shapes would 'speak back' to this speech and reveal another perspective. The movement for the beginning of the phrase was selected from the complementary responses to different aspects of the speech and then the rest of the movement was selected from the movement developed from the oppositional and in-between responses. Movement was initially selected to accentuate and simplify the relationship between the recorded spoken language and the movement in an attempt to create a parodic relationship between the two. For example, the movement that had been created for the word 'chicken' in the improvisation focusing on the vocabulary used was selected. This movement was made up of the performers using turn out, a flat back, upper arms fixed to the torso and outstretched lower arms and hands to provide a, comical image of a chicken.

The movement choreographed then clearly moves away from a complementary relationship with the recorded spoken language and offers other meanings. For example, when the soundtrack plays Janice's voice saying 'You can go into Sainsbury's or Tesco's and you can buy a chicken for £3. And you can eke out three meals out of that. You can have roast chicken. You can have soup and you can have sandwiches'. The movement changes from a heightened complementary parodic relationship to a more complex one. The language Janice uses is simple and patronizing, rejecting the complexity of the situation presented by previous speakers. Janice is offering extremely simple analysis and solutions. The movement translation here becomes more complex as the dancers become further entangled in their own body. At the words 'You can have roast chicken' their right arm moves in a curved pathway through the space coming to rest at an awkward and tense angle as the wrist bends to twist the position of the hand. With the phrase 'You can have soup' the performers' left arm moves into the space created by the right arm at the same time as the left knee and ankle bend while wrapping around the right leg. This inverted extension of the leg is pushed its limit. And as the phrase 'and you can have sandwiches' is uttered the performers' upper bodies attempt to move in a curved pathway to the right side of the space and the complex and entangled position results in them losing balance and falling to the floor. As they fall, the performers attempt to remain in this position but release their hands to catch their fall. In this example, the movement offers another meaning. The complexity of movement that accumulates to the point where the performers become unable to continue could offer the perspective that feeding a family on a low budget is more complex than buying a £3 chicken and finding inventive ways of making it last. When the movement and the recorded spoken language are presented in this double-voiced dialogue the viewer is able to view the different positions present and the dialogue between them. Here, the incongruity between the recorded spoken language and movement reminds the viewer of their active role in the production of meaning. Even though some of the movement diverged from a complementary relationship with the recorded spoken language, the process of creating all of the movement from this analysis of the speech meant that the movement did exist in a significant relationship with the recorded spoken language and even when the movement continues without the speaker, her interview continued to echo through the movement translation.

This approach experimented with allowing the movement translation to be of a greater length than the recorded spoken language, the aim being for the viewer to consider the effect of no longer hearing the source text, but still seeing the movement translation. This process also resonates with Tymoczko's (2007) reference to the Arabic tradition of accepting that a translator should add new meaning to the source text in their own translation. Thus, as well as playing with different and new meanings, the movement can add to the recorded spoken language when existing side by side, a process which allocates movement a central role in communicating to the viewer. While the recorded spoken language was never given exclusive performance time, the movement was.

An intricate and complex floor pattern was choreographed and each performer threw their apple in the air, having to move to a new space in order to catch another performer's apple. The performers also performed sections of the previous 'apple bitch' movement phrase to move around the space. This movement sequence was incredibly difficult to perform accurately and the choreographer asked the performers to continue repeating and rotating the sequence until one of the performers was not in position to catch their apple. When a performer missed their apple, the other performers would all watch that performer in stillness before ending the section by moving into the next phrase of movement. The aim of this continuation of the translation was to undermine the secure view of the position expressed in the interview material that good planning could prevent anyone falling into poverty and to present a moving image of a well-choreographed movement phrase that could be broken by one small change in force, directing or spacing by either the thrower or catcher.

Task 2: Bodies in Dialogue

This second task was developed by exploring ways of surrendering monolistic control over the text. This meant acknowledging that the choreographer needed to recognise and involve the performers in the translation process. Rather than just exploring my own choreographic translation process and bringing finished movement sequences or even motifs into the studio for the performers to learn and perform, my task was to create a series of choreographic tasks that would consider and develop a collaborative translation process. Just as Tymoczko (2009) noted that 'group translation methods' in China undermined the view of the single-author, the aim here became to explore ways of deepening the heteroglossia of the performance material by including the performers' positions and dialogue with the verbatim material, the choreographer and each other's bodies in both the translation process and product. This task also tried to reflect an awareness of Rabiger's (2004) assertion that the representation of documentary material can include personal 'impressions, perceptions and feelings'. Therefore, improvisational tasks were developed that attempted to include questions of who the translator was, what their position was in relation to the speaker of the speech and what their reaction was to the speech.

The first stage of the task developed asks the mover (A) to imagine the individual, whose interview is being played as a body in the space and dance with it, depending on how they feel about that body. For example, the mover could attack it (use their body or parts of their body to move through the space and as if coming into contact with the individual), support it (provide positions in which to take the imaginary weight of the individual), dance in unison with it (complement the rhythm, tone, etc. of the individual), silence it (attempt to find and throw the body out of the performance space or compress the body and hide or smother it with their own body or swallow the body), promote it (try to emphasise and project the individual out to the viewer).

The second stage of the task asks the mover (B) to consider their own response to the recorded interview and mover A's response. Mover B was then asked to physicalize their response by engaging in a physical dialogue with mover A's body. For example, mover B could attack it (use their body or parts of their body to collide with, block or change the direction of mover A's movement), support it (find ways to support the movement sequence for example providing contact and a base on which to support and take mover A's weight), dance in unison with it (perform in direct unison with mover A's movement), silence it (attempt to propel mover A's body out of the performance space or compress, smother or find another way to bring mover A to stillness), promote it (try to emphasise mover A's movement by lifting them up and elevating their position or re-positioning them somehow in the space to a more powerful position (i.e. Downstage Centre).

The third stage of this task asks mover C to reflect on and attempt to physicalize the dialogue between Mover A and Mover B. This response

Table 4.5 Bodies in dialogue

Stage 1	Mover A listens to voice and imaging the voice as an invisible body in the space begins to physicalize a personal response to the voice
Stage 2	Mover B listens to the voice and observes Mover A's response unfold until the extract has played once through. Mover B then begins to physicalize a personal response to Mover A's response
Stage 3	Mover C listens to the voice and observes Mover A and Mover B's response until the extract has played three times through. Mover C then attempts to physicalize their response to the relationship between the two bodies

must take the form of solo material that focuses on their understanding of the relationships at play between these bodies.

The audio recording of the interview is played so all can hear (Table 4.5).

In the creation stage, this task was applied in the translation of a speech extracted from an interview with a service user of 1624 Independent People, a young man aged 21 who explained his attempt to secure council accommodation after being made homeless and living in temporary hostel accommodation

Every week when I go to bid on Houses, it becomes like some stupid competition in my head. Me against all the other thousands of people that are waiting on a permanent property. It shouldn't be like that and to move up the ladder I have to prove how worthy I am. It's like I have to be like "I have been waiting this long", or "I have this disability" or "I have this many children". I have been trying to find a permanent property, but I just haven't found one. I do deserve somewhere (Table 4.6).

Example: Bidding

Mover A's translation of the material seemed to complement the speaker's explanation that it felt as if they were competing with a number of different people for each available property. Her huge leap backwards in the space when the speaker said 'I have this disability' could, for some people, communicate the fact that she felt this person should step out of the race. Mover B's reaction to Mover A's translation was incredibly forceful and at times aggressive. Her manipulation of Mover A's body in the space to become lower made Mover A appear ready for a more serious battle and the propelling of her body to use and cover more

Table 4.6 Bidding

Stage 1	Mover A listened to the speech and immediately began to gently move from side to side, with the heels of her feet slightly leaving the floor as if attempting a gentle jog but her toes were stuck to the floor. This movement was repeated throughout the entire speech and at the moments the speaker said 'I have this disability' she took a leap backwards. Throughout the phrase Mover A's head and focus moved between looking forwards and looking behind her
Stage 2	Mover B listens to the voice and observes Mover A's response unfold until the extract has played once through. Mover B then begins to physicalize a personal response to Mover A's response Mover B watched Mover A and before she was instructed to move she mirrored the steady shifting of Mover A's body. When allowed to respond Mover B ran directly to Mover A, used her upper arms to force her shoulders and upper body down and placed her hands on Mover A's hips and applied force to shift her further in the space, so her weight was moving between her feet. Next Mover B made contact with Mover A by placing her lower back just above Mover A's hips and ran backwards, forcing Mover A to move forwards in the space. Mover A tried to resume her posture and movement phrase of leaping back when the speech said 'I have this disability' but Mover B forcefully and determinedly repeated the manipulation of moving Mover A's upper body down and making her movements bigger and travel forwards
Stage 3	Mover C also unconsciously mirrored the shifting motion developed by Mover A while he watched the improvisation unfold. When given the instruction to move Mover C positioned himself in the exact position Mover B had positioned Mover A and shifted from side to side but moving further to each side than Mover B had managed to move Mover A. Mover C also moved forwards in the space and moved between movements where he suddenly moved forwards as if propelled by an outside force and slower contracted and dense movements that looked as though he was trying to fit through awkward and tight spaces. Mover C's focus constantly shifted to different levels and directions and gave the impression that he was looking at several different bodies in the space

space and move forwards communicated an anger at any translation that doesn't emphasis that every person has a right to, and a right to fight for, a decent and secure home. Mover C's translation of the dialogue between these two bodies was full of tension and although it was solo material, gave the sense of moving with and through lots of different bodies in the space.

Before the improvisation had finished, I asked the three performers to move into their own space and develop a solo phrase of material grounded in their experience of this improvisation. I then asked three more performers to choose one of the performers to stand near and pick up their phrase of movement. All of the three performers chose to pick up Mover C's movement phrase. I then choreographed a solo movement phrase for each performer that drew on the movement developed from each performer's contribution to this improvisation. Each of these solos moved forwards and backwards in the space. I then choreographed duets that used and developed the movement material created in the improvisation which moved between two people forcing their way past each other and helping their partner move forwards in the space.

Task 3: Choreographers Agency

Perteghella (2013) suggests that some creative or experimental translations such as her own experimental and mixed medium poetry translations, risk becoming unintelligible if the reader is not also shown the original text, making them 'aware of the translator's inevitable subjectivity within the text' and training the reader in 'reading experimental texts'. She offers the following thoughts on how a translation might attempt to address these issues within the text itself, without having to locate the readers of the text and train them in how to read translations.

> Of course, one way of including the non-specialist reader into understanding and enjoying creative translation is in fact to show its literary gestation, the drafting process, without being obsessed by the illusion of the 'polished, finished' product, and to encourage readers to read and view multiple versions of the same text. This clearly entails an understanding of how translation evolves and changes – shapeshifts – by literary publishers too. Further, the proliferation of e-books and digital reading devices could aid the publication of multimodal translations. (Perteghella 2013)

Perteghella's argument that translators' development of methods to reveal and include their 'drafting process' will draw the reader's attention to the fact that the translation process includes 'multiple versions of the same text', can be used as a starting point to consider how to develop performance material that will similarly reveal the choreographic process and focus the viewers' attention on the choreographic choices.

In addition to developing ways of generating movement material, choreographic structural devices were explored with the aim of developing a meta-narrative that reveals the choreographer's agency. During the entire workshop and creation period, approaches were explored for exposing the choreographer's (my own) social, economic and political position, as well as my role in the manipulation of material. In order to 'relinquish monolistic control' I wanted to find playful and creative ways in which to expose my own agency and manipulating role in an attempt to 'de-privilege' the self and produce performance material that allows meaningful dialogue to develop through a focus on the muddy and ambiguous nature of the meanings communicated.

The experimental choreographic studio-based process, during which the movement material is created, explored, re-worked, manipulated and structured, could be understood in the same way Loffredo and Perteghella (2008: 97) have depicted the translator's drafting process as a practice of self-writing 'whereby the 'self' writes and re-writes itself'. The concept of choreographing and re-choreographing the self and a personal response to the verbatim material in the choreographic process is a valid way to consider the process, but also offers possibilities for the performance material. Rather than choreographing one single movement sequence for each interview, possible ways of choreographing movement sequences that transform, repeat and break-down in order to find a way to embody the translation process were approached.

One example of experimenting with the inclusion of the choreographer's agency was the inclusion in the soundtrack of an interview spoken by myself (see DVD Chapter 3). The soundtrack included me speaking my recollection of the 1966 *Cathy Come Home*. This oral account of my memory of a moment in the film clearly includes my personal perception of the film text,

> My memory of the beginning of the film is of these gorgeous scenes where Reg tries to make Cathy laugh and she tries to suss him out. They go on a few dates and you watch them fall in love. And this one moment that sticks out, I think they climb up these stairs or something and Reg says [Soundtrack plays audio clip from the film of Reg saying 'well it's just us now, let's have some babies then'] and Cathy replies [soundtrack plays audio clip from the film of Cathy saying "I'd like that"]. And then everything happens really fast, we see them get married, move into somewhere, find out they are having a baby and just excited as I guess a lot of couples are about making a home together for the first time [soundtrack plays audio clip from film Cathy: 'I was scared Reg, I was really, I haven't got much courag' Reg: 'Well it's just us now Cath, just you and me, have some babies' Cathy: 'I'd like that Reg' Reg: 'Sod to all the rest']. And then just as quickly as you watch them fall in love, you see Reg, he

injures himself at work. He's off work for a few weeks and then they fall behind on their rent and then just because of that one moment, everything starts unravelling for them. And this always sticks out for me, that image of them, they know they are going to be evicted because they've fallen behind on rent and they gather all their belongings, and they board up the house and they are waiting as people knock down the door. It doesn't take long for people to get through Reg's planks that he's boarded up the door with, and they are through. And they are evicted from their home, with their belongings just taken out in front of them, in front of everyone watching.

As the soundtrack plays the choreographer's recalled memory, including an emotional response and a clearly stated view that Cathy and Reg's lives unravel suddenly due to unjust circumstances, the performers race around the stage moving swiftly between momentary tableaux that complement my description. The inclusion of my own memories and my own perceptions and feelings about the situation, while the performers clearly worked hard to keep up with and support my words, reminded viewers of my role as author of the performance text, thus making the viewer aware that any performance material is of course a 'refraction' of the authors voice, a result of heteroglossic material as identified by Bakhtin. The connection between movement and the spoken language, which had existed in a direct complementary relationship, starts to break down and the movement is clearly running at a time-lag behind the spoken words. This temporal split is designed to introduce the concept that the movement and recorded/spoken language exist as separate modes of communication. This section is interrupted by a recording of an extract from an interview collected with a service user at 1624 Independent People, spoken live by Preidel. The aim here was to draw attention to the fact that no one individual will be used to tell this story and that no one individual will ever get to finish their story.

Drafting Process

During the devising process, two different movement sequences were created as a response to the same speech, one using Task 1 and one using Task 2. The speech used as a starting point was an interview collected from a 19-year-old woman who had experienced homelessness and was now living in supported housing. The extract used from her interview is transcribed below:

The first time I really needed help with housing was when I'd been private renting for about a year. I couldn't pay my rent anymore and I got kicked out. Um, I first went to, to my landlord, well not the landlord but the people who worked for the landlord, the letting agency. And I went to them and I was like, 'Look, I've lost my job and I may not be able to pay my rent for a little while, so you know, can I have some leeway?' um and they were like 'We just need the rent by the end of the month you know?' and I was like 'okay, well maybe I'll have another job by then' and you know I kind of went 'okay well fair enough'. By then end of the month, I still hadn't found another job and I still couldn't pay my rent and they were like 'right we are going to kick you out, that's it' and I was like 'You can't just kick me out of your house. That's not fair, I have been trying to find work and I have been trying to find ways around it, I have been trying you know? There's nothing I can do now' I did try and find other places that would be cheaper to rent so then I could find work and pay back that rent and still have somewhere to live. But like that time I did try and find other ways around it. I went down to the council several times and I went to them and I said 'look I'm going to be kicked out of my flat in two days because I've lost my job, I'm completely screwed can you help me?' and the councils reply was that 'you know you're not actually homeless yet so there's nothing we can do for you' and I was like 'you can't just wait until I am actually on the streets to help me. I need somewhere to go now'.

The movement developed in the first task included Preidel walking calmly and freely across the whole stage space, occasionally performing movements that appeared to be in response to an external impulse, propelling part of her body backwards with a significant and strong force. Her body quickly recovered from the movement as she continued to move about the space performing the speech. Preidel is joined by two male performers Rowbottom and Ridley-DeMonick as they collect all of the objects on stage and put them into bin bags, also collecting Preidel and depositing her inside a bin bag. Again Preidel's movement remains relaxed and calm, climbing out to continue her open walk around the space.

The movement created in the second task is performed as a unison trio and includes fast and strong floor movement, incorporating a combination of spins, rolls and falls that build at a frantic pace. This movement also includes sudden changes in which the performers' weight is positioned in a way that shifts them in different directions, however this time the movement impulse appears to be an internal one. In performance, the movement created in the second task was performed by Preidel as she also performed the speech live, and the movement created in the first task was performed directly after by Preidel, Webber and Kindell as the soundtrack played a repetition and continuation of the speech Preidel had just performed, although this time the speech was heard in the original speaker's own voice. The accent, rhythm and tone of the two different performances of the same speech is significantly different and the viewer is asked to notice and remain aware of the difference between the original speakers voice and the performance of that interview. Through viewing these two different movement responses, the viewer is invited to consider the drafting process. The movement that accompanies this same speech is very different and offers different meanings. The calm pace and the recovery and re-centring of the performer after the sudden bursts of movement communicate a determined individual who is managing to stay in control. An alternative reading is that they are managing to pretend to be in control. The frantic and open movement of the second section could offer insight of an individual who has lost control and has internalised the chaos of being thrown out of their home. The first section offers a matter of fact tone, with a focus on recalling an experience, whereas the movement in section two offers an emotive response that places the performer in the event itself. This presentation of different movement with the same section of verbal language encourages the viewer to consider the different choices available to the choreographer in the creation of the movement response and also undermines any view that a correct movement response exists.

'Thanks'

Another way of including or performing the drafting process was by experimenting with presenting the same movement sequence with two different edits of the same speech. An interview with a housing officer during which she explains her own previous experience of homelessness is edited into two different versions. The first version is spoken live by Preidel, the transcript of which is below.

> It was the day I turned 16, I um guess I thought I was an adult. My mum's hours at work had been cut down and she wanted to move into a one bedroom flat. I thought that would be the perfect time to move in with my boyfriend. I got myself a part-time job, so I could pay half his bills and half his rent and still go to college and that. My mum did move, but

she moved further than I thought, she moved to Scotland and yeah I was happy in that flat

The second version is spoken live by Rowley, the transcript of which is below.

> It was the day I turned 16, I um guess I thought I was an adult. My mum's hours at work had been cut down and she wanted to move into a one bedroom flat. I thought that would be the perfect time to move in with my boyfriend. I got myself a part-time job, so I could pay half his bills and half his rent and still go to college and that. My mum did move, but she moved further than I thought, she moved to Scotland and yeah I was happy in that flat. About 7 months later, I was still happy at work and college, but I really hated living there. It or he, it just wasn't what I expected. I knew I had to go, I just didn't know where to go. I should have waited until I got a full-time job but I didn't I just left, walked out. Left all of my stuff. It's hard asking for help because you feel like a failure, that you've left yourself down. I really appreciate everyone helping me out though; I just wish I could have done it by myself

During the devising process, movement was created using Task 1, which resulted in a trio during which the performer performs the speech live while the movement changes from the mover moving independently to moments of support from the two male performers, to being lifted, shifted and moved through the space by giving full weight to the other bodies. The relationship between the speaker and the two movers is ambiguous. At times it appears they are supporting her in her journey, enabling her to stay upright and not fall, at times it appears they are inhibiting her own movement and forcing her pathway.

In performance, this trio was performed twice at two different points in the piece and by two different performers. The movement performed is exactly the same, however the first time it is performed by Preidel as she delivers the abridged version of the speech and then continues to perform the movement without the words. In the second performance by Rowley, she delivers the entire extract so that the words and movement start and end at the same point. The repetition of the same movement, but with different versions of the speech and performed by different performers encourages viewers to consider how the editing of interviews, including the choice of when to begin and end an extract, shapes their own reading of the performance material. The fact that in one performance the recorded/spoken language is left to resonate through the body as the movement translation continues, and in the other the movement begins and ends with its source text, demands that the viewer notices this device and is encouraged to consider what the movement adds to the communication of the ideas and concepts explored in the performance material. The first version allows the viewer to hear half of the extract and watch the movement translation continue. Having heard the first few lines of the words and then watched the movement, perhaps viewers have relied on the movement to fill in the rest of the story or add a layer to their understanding of the story. Watching it for a second time, having to view the movement in double-voice discourse with the words, may challenge their initial reading of the movement. Thus, the viewer is asked to reflect on their own individual process of 'reading' the movement.

Contact with the theories, provocations and questions explored by the translation scholars discussed in this chapter has enabled a significant shift in my choreographic practice. I have been able to explore some of the possible ways that verbal language and choreographed movement can come together in a double-voiced discourse in live performance and consider the potential to reveal and stage the choreographer's own agency. There are of course many theories located in translation studies that I was not able to include in my practice or this discussion. There is, therefore, much more to be explored at the boundaries of translation studies and dance and performance studies. For example, where can the practice of group translation processes, drafting processes and prismatic translation be pushed to in choreographic practice?

References

Bakhtin, M. (1981). Discourse in the Novel (translated from Russian by M. Holquist and C. Emerson). In M. Holquist (Ed.), *The Dialogic Imagination* (pp. 259–422). Austin: University of Texas Press.

Bassnett, S. (2006). Writing and Translating. In S. Bassnett & P. Bush (Eds.), *The Translator as Writer* (pp. 173–183). London and New York: Continuum.

Batchelor, K. (2008). Third Spaces, Mimicry and Attention to Ambivalence: Applying Bhabhian Discourse to Translation Theory. *The Translator, 14*(1), 51–70.

Bottoms, S. (2006). Putting the Document into Documentary: An Unwelcome Corrective? *The Drama Review, 50*(3), 56–68.

Cathy Come Home (BBC, 1966).
Cathy Come Home (Jess McCormack, 2012).
Grierson, J. (1966). The First Principles of Documentary. In F. Hardy (Ed.), *Grierson on Documentary* (p. 147). London: Faber & Faber.
Halliday, M. A. K. (1978). *Language as Social Semiotic, the Social Interpretation of Language and Meaning*. London: Edward Arnold.
Halliday, M. A. K., & Hasan, R. (1989). *Language, Context and Text: A Social-Semiotic Perspective*. Oxford: Oxford University Press.
Halliday, M. A. K., McIntosh, A., & Strevens, P. (1964). *The Linguistic Sciences and Language Teaching*. London: Longmans.
Laban, R. (1971). *The Mastery of Movement* (3rd ed.). Boston, MA: Plays.
Loffredo, E., & Perteghella, M. (Eds.). (2006). *Translation and Creativity: Perspectives on Creative Writing and Translation Studies*. London: Continuum.
Loffredo, E., & Perteghella, M. (Eds.). (2008). *One Poem in Search of a Translator: Rewriting 'Les Fenetres' by Apollinaire*. Bern: Peter Lang.
O'Sullivan, C. (2012). Playing with(out) the Dictionary: Using Constrained Literature in the Development of Transferable Skills for Translators. *The Interpreter and Translator Trainer, 6*(2), 237–263.
Perteghella, M. (2013). Notes on the Art of Text Making. *The Creative Literary Studio* [Blog]. Available at: https://thecreativeliterarystudio.wordpress.com/tag/manuela-perteghella/. Accessed 6 Jan 2014.
Rabiger, M. (2004). *Directing the Documentary* (4th ed.). Amsterdam: Elsevier.
Renov, M. (1993). Toward a Poetics of Documentary. In M. Renov (Ed.), *Theorising Documentary* (pp. 12–36). London: Routledge.
Rogers, S. (2012). Homelessness Jumps by 14% in a Year. *The Guardian* [online]. Available at: http://www.theguardian.com/society/2012/mar/08/homelessness-jumps-repossession-unemployment. Accessed 10 Mar 2012.
Tymoczko, M. (2007). *Enlarging Translation, Empowering Translators*. Manchester: St Jerome Publishing.
Tymoczko, M. (2009). Why Translators Should Want to Internationalize Translation Studies. *The Translator, 15*(2), 401–421.

CHAPTER 5

Concluding Comments: Choreographed Dialogue

Abstract McCormack provides a summary of the arguments explored in the book by bringing together dance and performance studies theory and translation theory to deepen an analysis of the encounter between words and movement in physical/dance theatre performances. She offers a reflection that the combination of recorded/spoken language and movement is a powerful method of unsettling any concept of a single perspective, even more so when the performance material includes and exposes the choreographer/performers' agency. 'Choreographed Dialogue' explores ways to understand, articulate and engage in the process of choreographing movement as a response to verbatim spoken language.

Keywords Choreography · Dialogue · Verbatim theatre · Physical theatre

During my time as a dance-maker, performer and scholar working between dance and theatre departments, I have developed a particular interest in the encounter between spoken words and choreography. I am interested in how these two things come together in performance, the rehearsal room and the classroom but also in how we use both verbal language and movement to communicate in everyday life. In considering theories located in translation studies and the dialectic between theory and practice, this book crosses the boundaries between translation and dance studies and has aimed to ask questions about how we as dance-makers, scholars and students can employ the framework of translation to understand, and engage in the process of choreographing movement as a response to spoken language. My focus here has been on the interplay between movement and spoken word in verbatim theatre, however, it is my hope that this book will inspire the many scholars and practitioners already interested in the coming together of different texts and choreography to consider this encounter through the framework of translation in order to consider the numerous possibilities of this relationship.

A focus on staging the choreographer's editorial agency and an understanding of what Bakhtin (1981) refers to as dialogized heteroglossia has been at the centre of the arguments explored in this book. The choreographic practice discussed in Chapter 4 was driven by the understanding that a piece of performance work which acknowledges and enables different, perhaps conflicting, positions to co-exist prevents the presentation of any one authoritative or absolute position. The reason I was initially drawn to verbatim theatre as a choreographer was my belief that artwork of any kind cannot and should not present any absolute positions. As I noted in the Preface to the book, novelist Chimamanda Ngozi Adichie (2009) warns of the dangers of telling or consuming 'single stories' in the realm of fiction, media or personal relationships, which have the result in closing off the possibility of complex understanding. In poetic agreement with Bakhtin (1981), Ngozi Adichie argues that:

> The consequence of the single story is this: It robs people of dignity. It makes our recognition of our equal humanity difficult. It emphasizes how we are different rather than how we are similar…when we reject the single story, when we realize that there is never a single story about any place, we regain a kind of paradise.

This research process has uncovered a personal understanding that just seeking to include and present other people's words on stage is not enough to rupture this concept of a single story. At the end of this research process, Ngozi Adichie's statement resonates with Young's (2009: 72) assertion that verbatim theatre can either seek to record or report. Through trying to question and move beyond DV8 Physical Theatre's opening projected statement 'These are their words' (*To Be Straight With You*) and Soans' assertions that verbatim theatre audiences 'become' (2008: 23) the person who collected the interview, the practice as research took up the challenge of finding ways to avoid trying to record the material, but remained focused on trying to report. Perhaps it can be argued that, for verbatim theatre practitioners, Ngozi Adichie's paradise might be attained by approaching the performance process with an acknowledgement that verbatim theatre can in no way omit or erase the choreographer/director/writer/performer's presence and subjectivity and that, by making evident the editing choices, choreographic decisions and processes used in the work, they can hopefully invite the audience to also reject any single story and consider the complexity of the material presented.

For a practice that is fascinated with the translation of recorded/spoken verbal language into movement, it is notable that choreographers in the field of verbatim dance-theatre have had little contact with the field of translation studies. When this specific choreographic process is viewed as a translation process, from speech to body, from verbal language to corporeal text, then those concepts in translation studies which explore translation practice as a process of dialogue between translator and source text become pertinent and provide new ways to understand, articulate and participate in this choreographic practice. By combining an understanding and application of translation studies with experimental choreographic practice, this book sought to uncover ways of developing what Bakhtin (1981) refers to as dialogised heteroglossia when creating verbatim dance-theatre. By recognising their own role as author and editor of the performance material and developing ways of challenging the notion that they are neutral carriers of others' voices, verbatim theatre practitioners can avoid creating what Bakhtin refers to as the monoglossic performance material. The combination of recorded/spoken language and movement is a powerful method of unsettling any concept of a single perspective, even more so when the performance material includes and exposes the choreographer/performer's agency. Commentary provided by verbatim theatre practitioners is too often restricted by having to portray the director/writer/choreographer's role as neutral translators. *Cathy Come Home* (2012) attempted to expose the choreographer translator's agency, and developed reflexive choreographic tasks that found ways for the movement to explicitly speak back to the verbatim material. This provided the viewer with visibly constructed performance material, allowing them to produce readings based on their own interpretation of what was presented, reinforcing the impossibility of a simplistic and unambiguous explanation for the UK's rising homelessness statistics. By including two modes of communication (the spoken word and its movement translation) and placing them next to each other in performance, the practice was able to explore how to undermine the dominance of the spoken word in expressing meaning in theatre and to question the ability of either mode alone to fully communicate meaning, thus highlighting the polysemous nature of meaning. By exploring movement approaches, which attempt to focus on the dialogue between different and opposing perspectives, no unified or single-voiced language was allowed to develop and the monoglossia is interrupted and ambiguous, prompting a variety of readings.

This application of translation theories and practices to verbatim dance-theatre can offer a way for verbatim dance-theatre practitioners to recognise and incorporate their own editorial agency. By experimenting with ways to include and perform the choreographic process and agency, methods were produced that exposed, played with and developed a meta-narrative of the choreographer as translator. This produced performance material that invited the viewer to consider the space in which the dialogue between the translator and verbatim material occurred. By means of this experimental process, *Cathy Come Home* was able to strengthen understanding of ways in which to approach the production of performance material that can be understood as 'dialogized heteroglossia'. Bakhtin uses both the example of physical language and the use of 'language' taken from many different members of a society as examples of ways in which to achieve 'dialogized heteroglossia'. He comments on clowning's use of physical language and suggests it is a way of questioning and 'ridiculing all 'languages' and dialects' (1981: 273). *Cathy Come Home* included, and gave equal importance to, the movement and verbal language as a means of strengthening an understanding of movement as a valid and rich mode of communication and as a means of questioning the implicit centralising of a verbal language present in much mainstream verbatim theatre. This research, based around the intersection of the spoken word and its movement translation, as well as the meeting point of the verbatim recorded interviews and the translation, the self and the other, is concerned with the dialogue between these different bodies and experimented with exercises that included antagonistic approaches to translating the text, for example, responding through parody. Through this studio-based experimental practice, *Cathy Come Home* presented a combination of verbatim recorded/spoken language and their movement translation which positioned the translator in a dialogic context. The performance material encompassed the choreographer and performers' attempts to respond to and engage the verbatim interviews in a meaningful dialogue. The project empowered the choreographic translation process to be part of the creative and expository transformation of its source text (verbatim material) into something new and valid.

The performance material contained interviews, choreography and ideas taken from different sources, including those of different artists (Sanford, Loach, choreographer, performers), as well as a range of interviews from different members of society (individuals from different classes, generations, political positions and cultures). No single individual, perspective or mode of communication was allowed to dominate as the performance material consistently undermined and ruptured any sense of a unitary language. The choreographic processes which were developed placed an emphasis on exposing the dialogue between the different modes of communication used, thus producing material that demanded the viewer collaborate in the construction of meaning. *Cathy Come Home* used conflict, contradiction and multi-voiced discourse throughout the piece to comment on the complexity of the issue of homelessness. Images of entangled bodies desperately trying and failing to stay upright collide with the assured recorded interview of a journalist simplistically detailing the financial discipline required to escape poverty. Choreography moving between weight sharing and manipulation sits ambiguously next to the spoken words of a woman reflecting on how support services aided her escape from homelessness. These tensions between the recorded/spoken language and choreography served as a constant reminder of the polysemous and negotiable nature of meaning and echoed the underlying contradictions that exist in the discourse (political, social, media) surrounding the UK's increasing levels of homelessness.

The boundary between movement and verbal language as two modes of communication collapses as the two come together to present a performance of past events (the interview conducted by the artist in the academic's office, the debate between the journalist and the mother on BBC Radio 4, the mediated conversation between a support worker and her service user or the vox pop interviews conducted on the street) and the live event (the live performance combining verbatim recorded/spoken language and movement). It can be valuable for verbatim theatre practitioners to explore the possibilities of producing performance material that contains 'competing definitions for the same thing' (Bakhtin 1981: 427) and to stage the 'hostile relationships' (Batchelor 2008: 64) that can exist between source and target texts. This book has explored some ways for verbatim theatre practitioners to think about the staging of their drafting processes and include collaborative creative processes to generate performance material. The devising methods explored in this study are by no means exhaustive but do provide verbatim theatre practitioners and translators with some new ways to consider and perform their own agency. In this way, the notion of a single meaning is rejected in favour of a complicated and ambiguous response to events. It is precisely this double-voiced presentation of the spoken word and choreographed movement that helps to establish a complex and heterogeneous translation of the verbatim material. Through the creation of choreographic techniques which expose and include the choreographer's agency in the heteroglossic performance material, methods are revealed which enable a fundamental distancing from Soans' (2008: 23) understanding of verbatim theatre practice as the simple action of collecting spoken words from one location and transferring these exact words to a performance venue, thus allowing the audience to 'become' (ibid.) the person who heard and recorded these words when they were first spoken.

In addition to offering verbatim dance-theatre practitioners ways to include self-reflexive performance material that incorporates the editorial choices of a single choreographer, I started to explore approaches for collaborative or group choreographic translation process. Perhaps more significant than the development of approaches to stage my own agency was the development of choreographic exercises that explored group translation processes with a specific focus on the dialogue between different dancers. This approach, which called for dancers to respond to both their own and others' positions on the source text, offers the potential to stage the dialogue and tensions between these different and often conflicting positions. This multi-vocal and conversational approach to verbatim dance-theatre was an exciting space to explore and, [in a field which is defined by its inclusion of others' positions], this approach offers significant possibilities for the expansion of verbatim choreography. During the practical enquiry, this exploration, development and application of collaborative choreographic devices significantly altered my understanding and approach to verbatim dance-theatre practice and I hope that my future practice will include further exploration of these approaches. It would be interesting to investigate the possibilities of collaborative choreographic translation practice, and the development of performance material made entirely through this multi-vocal and conversational approach.

Although my own experimental studio-based research uncovered some possible means of making visible the editorial decisions and choreographic choices and processes used, an area of further practice as research could be to explore additional options for making these processes evident to an audience. This further practice as research could experiment with staging these choreographic processes, rather than only allowing them to occur in the rehearsal space, in order to then construct finished and rehearsed performance material. This exploration could offer further possibilities for the audience to enter into dialogue with the [physical/choreographic] translation process. Collected interview material could be played to a live audience, the choreographer and performers could make live editorial decisions regarding selection of verbal source material and experiment with choreographic material in front of a live audience. This way of creating the work, which exposes the subjective editorial and choreographic decisions, has the potential to further engage the audience in considering how the material is representing/responding to and transforming the source material. Another area of further practice as research could cast the audience themselves as collaborators in the editorial and/or choreographic process. Rather than focusing on ways to explore and expose the choreographer/performer's performance making processes the audience could be invited to make editorial and choreographic decisions themselves, allowing them another perspective from which to view the editorial and choreographic decisions in creating the verbatim dance-theatre material.

The initial aim for this book was simple. I wanted to explicitly set up a format for thinking about choreography for verbatim theatre by exploring the boundaries between translation studies and choreographic practice. I have argued throughout this book that drawing on theories, practices and provocations located in translation studies offer dance-makers, scholars and students with ways in which to consider the complexities and possibilities for the relationship between spoken words and choreographed movement. Contact with translation studies has transformed my own choreographic practice as my work as a performance scholar. I hope that this book inspires scholars, practitioners and students to ask further questions about the numerous possibilities at the intersection between translation and choreography.

References

Bakhtin, M. (1981). Discourse in the Novel (translated from Russian by M. Holquist and C. Emerson). In M. Holquist (Ed.), *The Dialogic Imagination* (pp. 259–422). Austin: University of Texas Press.

Batchelor, K. (2008). Third Spaces, Mimicry and Attention to Ambivalence: Applying Bhabhian Discourse to Translation Theory. *The Translator, 14*(1), 51–70.

Cathy Come Home (Jess McCormack, 2012).

Ngozi Adiche, C. (2009). *Chimamanda Ngozi Adichie: The Danger of a Single Story* [Video file]. Retrieved from: https://www.ted.com/talks/chimamanda_adichie_the_danger_of_a_single_story. Accessed 17 Nov 2012.

Soans, R. (2008). Robin Soans. In W. Hammond & D. Steward (Eds.), *Verbatim Verbatim: Contemporary Documentary Theatre*. London: Oberon Books.

Young, S. (2009). Playing with Documentary Theatre: Aalstand Taking Care of Baby. *New Theatre Quarterly, 25*, 72–87.

Index

A
Adaptation, 1, 6–14, 16, 97
Agency, 32, 38, 43, 48, 50–52, 55, 86, 93, 94, 111, 112, 114, 117, 120–122, 124

B
Bakhtin, Mikhail, 2, 13, 16–19, 22, 28, 37, 38, 39, 43, 48, 73, 75, 80, 86, 87, 93, 94, 96, 98, 113, 120–122, 124
Bassnett, Susan, 6, 7, 90
Bausch, Pina, 2, 3, 13, 65–67, 72
Berger, John, 5
Blythe, Alecky, 32, 33, 36, 37, 41, 55

C
Choreography, 3–6, 9, 12–16, 19, 20, 22, 28, 39–41, 57, 64, 67, 69, 72, 73, 77, 84, 119, 120, 123–125

Creativity, 5, 28, 29, 33, 43, 48–50, 55, 56, 58, 81, 82, 84
Cunningham, Merce, 65

D
Dance-theatre, 1–3, 5–10, 12–16, 18–20, 27, 28, 38, 39, 51, 54–56, 58, 59, 65, 69, 78, 81, 86, 90, 121, 122, 124, 125
Dancing, 15, 40, 74
Devising, 3, 9, 10, 14, 15, 52, 67, 76, 95, 113, 116, 124
Dialogue, 6, 10, 16, 17, 21, 28, 30, 35, 38, 47, 49, 52, 56–58, 73, 75–77, 91, 94, 98, 100, 106–108, 110, 112, 121–125
Documentary film, 43–47, 49, 52–54, 58
Double-voiced, 13, 16, 17, 19, 20, 27, 38, 54, 55, 58, 71, 75, 77, 85, 86, 94, 106, 117, 124
Dramaturgy, 8, 70

INDEX

DV8 Physical Theatre, 2, 3, 5, 10, 20, 63, 64, 120

H
Hare, David, 30, 35, 53
Heteroglossia, 16–19, 28, 38, 43, 48, 54, 73, 80, 86, 93, 94, 96, 98, 108, 120–122

I
Improvisation, 20, 59, 67–69, 92, 99, 102–105, 110, 111

M
Movement, 1–10, 12, 15, 16, 18–22, 27–29, 38–41, 43, 48, 49, 52, 54, 56–59, 63–81, 84–87, 90, 92, 94–108, 110–117, 119–125

O
O'Sullivan, Carol, 29, 48, 49, 54, 76, 77, 81–84, 94, 95

S
Soans, Robin, 29–31, 33–35, 37, 38, 43, 53, 120, 124

T
Translation, 1–3, 5–16, 19–22, 27–29, 38, 40, 41, 43, 48–52, 54–58, 63, 70–73, 75–79, 81–87, 90, 92, 94–96, 98, 99, 104, 106–112, 117, 119–125
Tymoczko, Maria, 6, 11, 14, 49–52, 54–58, 75–77, 92, 94, 95, 107

V
Vardimon, Jasmin, 3, 4
Verbatim theatre, 22, 27–31, 34–39, 41–44, 48, 51–59, 70, 75, 86, 94, 120–125